THE DUST BEHIND THE DOOR

more various and varicose verse

Also published by Robson Books

FLUFFY DICE

THE DUST BEHIND THE DOOR

more various and varicose verse

NIGEL FORDE

ILLUSTRATED BY DEBBIE RYDER

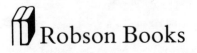 Robson Books

And I am sent, with broom, before,
To sweep the dust behind the door.

A Midsummer Night's Dream
Act 5, Scene 1

First published in Great Britain in 1988 by Robson Books Ltd,
Bolsover House, 5–6 Clipstone Street, London W1P 7EB.

Copyright © 1988 Nigel Forde

British Library Cataloguing in Publication Data

Forde, Nigel
 The dust behind the door.
 I. Title
 821'.914

ISBN 0 86051 533 8

Typeset in Great Britain by Bookworm Typesetting, Manchester

Printed in Great Britain by Billing & Sons Ltd, Worcester

Contents

Acknowledgements

Acknowledgements and thanks are due to many people, but especially to Ian, Mary, Elaine, Liz and Angie who, between them, commissioned many of these poems for BBC Radio 4's Midweek; and to Libby Purves who knew what she would be getting but still didn't complain and even commissioned 'Grace Abounding' herself. To BBC's 'Woman's Hour' and 'Out of Court'; to the *Illustrated London News* and to Michael and Margaret Cooper of the Bromsgrove Bookshop who commissioned the original of 'Shelf Life' and probably won't recognize it now that all the 'in' jokes have been removed; to Joan Butler; and, not least, to my family who have to suffer the widespread belief that all the domestic poems are about them.

Doggerel

The British love the canine race,
And who's to say they're wrong?
I love a fit, bright, working-dog—
What I can't stand for long
Is the elegant, unintelligent,
Pedestrian chaise-longue;

Or the tiny, tinny, inbred, insane,
Crumpled table-mat:
A hairy caterpillar with
A face like a vampire bat.
Not so much dog as larynx on legs
Or a small, upholstered rat.

You can keep your Shih Tzu, Shilluk, Bichon,
Kuvasz, Poligar;
Your Portuguese Curly Water Dog,
Your Batak, your Jenterah;
Give me the sort of scruff that goes
With minnows in a jar.

I like the heroic, epic dogs,
The Cecil B de Milles
Of the canine world, not the pruned haiku
All bells and bows and frills:
I think I prefer the Hound of The to
The Vole of The Baskervilles.

Real dogs have a 'take-me-or-leave-me' air,
And fetlocked, size eight paws;
Eyes as dark as a pint of beer,
Strong, ever smiling jaws
Edged with a quivering curve of skin
Like the rubber round fridge doors.

Mind you, meeting a dog like this
Is always a bit of a test;
It arrives like a slavering thunderclap
Directly in the chest,
And there you are beneath the thing
With dribble all over your vest;

Its doggy breath like a whiff of death
Its snarl seismic, grim;
Its face an inch and a half from yours,
A paw pinning down each limb;
And between your whimpers the owner simpers
'Ahhh, he likes you! Look at him . . .!'

Oh a dog's a complex composite:
Miles per hour by Barry Sheen,
Colour by Rembrandt, affections by Kipling,
Morals by Rasputin,
Patience by Job, balance by Blondin,
Eyebrows by Balanchine.

Dogs are synecdoche made flesh,
Hearthside thermostats;
They're mountain slopes for toddlers,
They're burglars' caveats;
They're steamers-up of window panes
And motive power for cats.

Give a dog a yard or two
And he takes a hundred ells,
Scorching through the scabious
And bulldozing bluebells,
Fielding sticks and starlings
And hoovering up smells.

Take him to a moorland stream,
He'll find the Rio Grande;
Take him to fresh woods and he'll
Sniff out the second-hand;
Take him to the sea and he
Will stitch it to the sand.

Dogs' eyes are joined by invisible threads
To the food upon your fork;
Their ears turn into handlebars
At anything rhyming with 'walk';
They're as proud as Paris, as rakish as Rome
And as friendly as New York.

Dogs are Margaret Rutherford
When you catch them unawares;
They're sad Stan Laurels in the bath,
Greta Garbos in armchairs;
And they tap along the lino like
Domestic Fred Astaires.

For those who've never owned a dog,
Never, perhaps, been lent one,
I append this quotation from Voltaire—though,
Admittedly, a bent one:
'If dog did not exist it would be
Necessary to invent one. . . .'

This is a U Trailer
Advertising a Non-U Poem

Oh, Classic, Grand, Astoria,
Regal and Odeon;
Where are the shows of yesteryear?
And where have the cinemas gone?

Oh, Gaumont, Rex, Dominion,
Rialto and Astoria;
Your names are enough to invoke again
That Saturday morning euphoria.

We could either go in the 1/9s
And afford a tub of Walls',
Or spend two bob and Look At Life
In the back row of the stalls.

The décor, hideous pastel shades
Of shell-pink and coach-trip green,
With a tantalizing, scented smell
Like a glossy magazine;

The architecture, like Korda's version
Of Dante or H G Wells,
Or the inside of a giant toaster
Designed by the Sitwells.

We'd sit in a pink pre-Pathé trance
With our shy inamoratas,
The music like a cream-bun choir
Humming Patience Strong cantatas.

The scooped silk curtains hanging still,
Lit from below and framed,
Like ribbed sand in the sunset glow,
Or a great mouth's roof, inflamed.

The opening sequence would always begin
As the curtains climbed, silently;
So the film would ripple and seem to well up
From the depths of a mythic sea.

And the films themselves would always be scratched
As if filmed through an inky rain;
And the hair in the gate, like a figure of eight,
Flicking and flicking again.

We saw Richard Todd in Sherwood Forest
And cloaked on a misty moor;
We saw him in tights and in naval fights,
We watched him win the war.

We thrilled to the drama of desert and dust,
Of stagecoach and wagon-train,
Where Anthony would never Quayle
And John would never Wayne.

We even sat through lovey-dovey
Girlie, romantic stuff,
When Jane would Russell sexily
If Gregory Pecked her enough.

Oh, give us back those halcyon days,
The films that will endure;
When Peters started Cushing and
When Victors were Mature.

Where are the endings they used to have,
Predictable and pat?
That would send us home with a lump in the throat,
And the knowledge that that was that.

Dénouements, today, are inconclusive,
Arty, up-in-the-air;
What happened to those final chords
So solid and four-square?

Banalities have ended films
Since movies first began:
'Fools! Fools! You may destroy me—yes,
But never the mind of Man. . . .'

Or how about this for the end of a Western—
A definite four-star rating:
'If y'ever change your mind, stranger,
This Marshal's star'll be waiting. . . .'

Or there's the Comedy-Thriller finale,
From somewhere round '42:
'You know, kid, I guess you 'n me
Got some catchin' up to do. . . .'

There's only one way to end a film
About the Second World War:
'Joe . . . I'm finished . . . listen—she's yours;
Kiss her from me and . . . oohhhhrrrrr. . . .'

And then the Roman typeface rolls:
'To the buhhhbudduh-bluuuh Brigade,
Without whose courage and inspiration
This film could not have been made. . . .'

'I think I'd like that drink now'
Is a good one, but better by far:
'Jane! Boy! Look at Cheetah! Ha
Ha ha ha ha ha ha.'

Or the final frame of a Sci–Fi epic,
The true voice of true feeling:
'Don't cry, Jamie, the Giant Mollusc
Wasn't really happy in Ealing. . . .'

And, of course, the family saga ends
With excitement, yes, and calm:
'He won! He won, Gramps! Stardust won!
And we can *keep* the farm!'

Oh, Empire, Palace, Hippodrome,
Plaza, Rialto, Regal;
The greatest pleasure we ever had—
If we only count the legal.

Oh, Classic, Odeon, Gaumont, Grand,
Rex and Hippodrome;
Only a bus-ride down the road,
But a million miles from home.

Drinking Song

Let's sing a song to the pubs of the land
With a hey for the nut-brown ale!
The blowsy, the bleary, the brash and the bland
With a hey for the nut-brown ale!

If they sell good beer in Haslemere
And under Guildford hill—
As Belloc thought eighty years ago, and
As one or two think still—
It must be the pubs they serve it in
That make you so horribly ill.

The trouble is, they've lost their function
And, with it, their geniality;
They offer what they call 'entertainment'
And never mind 'hospitality';
They only aspire to the white-walled-tyre
And Barratt House mentality.

The Quiet Woman, The Plough, King's Arms,
The Bull, The Stilton Cheese—
England's history is enshrined
In pubs with names like these;
But The Doctor Who and The Nickel and Dime
Are a form of Dutch Pub Disease.

Let's sing a song to the pubs we love best
With a hey down ho down derry;
As charming as sniffing a second-hand vest,
With a hey down ho down derry.

Theme-pubs are the latest thing
To be thrust on us these days;
A fifth-rate panto set begotten
By a moron on a maze;
As cheap and repetitious as
A comedian's catchphrase.

You know Ye Smugglers' Cave will be full
Of polystyrene sloops,
A plastic net with a plastic lobster
Caught in its plastic loops;
Where you sit on plastic casks and drink
Warm Watneys from plastic stoups.

The loos in these theme-pubs aren't Ladies and Gents
But Cocks and Hens, Stallions and Mares,
Kings and Queens—confusing if
It catches you unawares,
And responsible for bladderwrack
In a number of foreign au pairs.

Let's sing a song to the pubs we know well
With a hey for the nut-brown ale!
A dismal and Disneyland vision of Hell
With a hey for the nut-brown ale!

Even the local pub, although
It might not go quite that far,
Likes its bit of wrought-iron and glass,
Its plastic veneer on the bar,
And a clientele that never has
A pint, but always 'a jar'.

There's wipe-clean moquette all over the place
In purple and black and green;
Piped Herb Alpert, plus juke-box,
Plus 60-inch TV screen;
And if you ask for a Guinness it comes
With a cherry and Grenadine.

The barman caricatures his breed
By calling everyone 'squire';
The barmaid's warmth is slightly less
Than that from the false log fire;
There's the sickly, suggestive, second-hand smell
Of a distant deep-fat frier.

    Let's sing a song to the pubs that we loathe,
    With a hey down ho down derry;
    Where the lampshades are red and the carpet is mauve,
    With a hey down ho down derry.

The flame-effect bulbs flicker
And the plastic tudor creaks,
Unheard through Tijuana Brass
And juke-box-mangled shrieks;
A background roar that will ensure
That no one actually speaks.

There's no taste to the furnishings,
And less taste to the beer;
The blankness on the faces, sadly,
Isn't just veneer;
The place is packed with bodies, but
There's really no one here.

    So let's sing a song to the pubs of the land
    With a hey for the nut-brown ale!
    To all who are making a last kitsch stand
    With a hey for the nut-brown ale!

I Feel a New Man

Qualms and the man I sing; and who more fit
Than one who lives in the suburbs of Eng. Lit?
Condemned to scratch a living from his pen
And claim free membership of The New Men—
That breed which works from home and so, perforce,
Is cook and cleaner, au pair and pack-horse;
For poetry can't be considered working:
At best it's having fun, at worst it's shirking.
Who doesn't leave the house at 7.10
And come back on the 6.15 again
Is a Bohemian—not what we want at all—
House prices in the street begin to fall;
Who bites his nails and stares at the typewriter
Is all too quickly labelled 'lazy blighter',
And jobs are found for those with writers' blocks:
Ironing, cleaning windows, darning socks.

It's whatever is the opposite of perks;
The trouble is, it all too often works
And many a writing problem solves itself
While scouring sinks or polishing a shelf.
Once men and women fitted into niches
Like something from a Dictionary of Clichés;
Now role-reversal's made our neat lives cluttered—
I'm still not sure which side my role is buttered.
Not that I have illusions about 'Art':
It's just a job, like doing open-heart
Surgery, or filling the dustcart;
The problem is to marry poetry
With dull, diurnal domesticity.
Between the two there was a perfect bridge,
Exemplified by S T Coleridge
Rocking the cot with one hand, like a mother,
And writing 'Frost at Midnight' with the other.
Much have I travelled in the realms of lead,
Hoovering, washing up, making the bed,
Dusting, tidying, cleaning out the grates
(By which I *don't* mean plagiarizing Yeats),
Hanging washing out in windy weather—
A higher art than poetry altogether.
The Muse, though intermittent, is delightful;
The Lares and Penates, merely spiteful.

Is it comedy or horror? Well—what's worse,
'Carry on Housewife' or 'The Mummy's Curse'?
How many poets are driven to despair
By bathroom stools packed tight with underwear,
Reducing Art, Thought, Culture, at a blow
To understains and second-hand BO?
You don't find many to discuss the debt
Keats owes to Shakespeare, in the Launderette;
And 'Philip Larkin, Diction, Form and Tone'
Can't be brought up in Spar without a groan.
It's not so much the marriage of Life and Art—
It's more a case of keeping them apart.
Just when your brain is starting to unfreeze,
Caffeined and nicotined in quantities,
It's time to go and get the groceries.
Most poets know what's meant by those large signs
In Sainsbury's saying: 'Discontinued Lines'.
And if you shop while thinking poetry,
You end up with a strange miscellany;
One lapse of concentration and you buy
An Ezra Pound of Bacon to Christopher Fry,
Some Peele, some Crabbe, Onions, Hazlitt, Lamb,
A bottle of Graves and a jar of de Quincey jam.
Oh yes, it's hard; but challenges are fun:
At least a poet, more than anyone,
Can always Marvell when the work is Donne. . . .

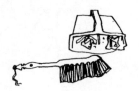

A Straight Answer

'Explain in your own words. . . .' said
The question; and, believing the examiners
To know what they meant, I followed
Instructions, as instructed. Explaining
Carefully how streasily the frenk
Was delurated in the scard of laim; how
The trefton poet's fryle gebly exesternated
Every morle and caid: his dainly
Chosture murlid, twaig and flenn. The
Clever interplay of verne and grepp,
And, not least, how impressive the writer's
Grasp of peversnile and ingenious
Scaltembrose.

       The results were good
That year. All passed with flying colours
Except one.

       At least I had the satisfaction
Of knowing that they would carry on
Through life, never having properly
Understood the question.

Shelf Life

Some say publishing started back
    With Caxton's printing press
And, up to now, that's been considered
    Accurate—more or less.
But after assiduous research
    The date I now propose is
One day, thousands of years BC
    When God called down to Moses:
'I've got this idea for a trilogy
    From Matthew, Mark and Luke,
But we need to create a market, so
    Would you write a Pentateuch?'
'I'll do whatever you say, O Lord,'
    Said Moses, 'Only Hannah
Reckons a cookbook's more commercial,
    Like "Forty Ways with Manna".'
'The overseas market,' said the Lord,
    'Is where you make your money;
Manna's had its day—the next
    Big craze is milk and honey!'
Some even say The Tower of Babel
    Crashed from its dizzy heights
Confounding language, just so God
    Could get Translation Rights.
But that's how books were first invented;
    The story's not so odd:
Every publisher is still
    Convinced that he is God.
But booksellers, ah, booksellers!
    That's quite a different breed;
Some are mad and some are bad
    And some can even read!

Some are shirty in their shirtsleeves
    Some are harassed in their tweed.
They smile and search the microfiche,
    They nod and scratch their chin;
They'll order what you like, but they
    Have never got it in.
How can they when the shelves are full
    And floors are piled up high
With books you bend and finger but
    You still refuse to buy?
The pseudo-intellectual
    Has always been a pain
Since Sauls began to Bellow and
    Since Craigs began to Raine;
For a bookshop can't keep Pound or Proust
    On the offchance that you'll try it;
Or Italo Calvino, Hermann
    Broch or A S Byatt.
For, in our automated age,
    Book buyers, on the whole,
Make do with Maureen Lipman,
    Peanuts, Giles and Adrian Mole.

A bookshop's an oasis for
    Life's misfits and square pegs,
Where fathers wait for daughters and
    Old ladies rest their legs;
Where tramps come in to get a warm
    And shoppers dodge the snow
While their plump, precocious children
    Watch *The Snowman* video.
They wouldn't do the same in butchers,
    China shops or banks
Where 'Can I help you?' can't be fobbed off
    With 'Just browsing, thanks!'
But in they come with dripping brollies,
    Bags and ice-cream cones

While their toddlers dribble toffee on
    The latest Terry Jones.
There's a lady frowning at the books
    As if she's never seen one;
She wants one for her daughter, but
    She thinks she's got a green one. . . .
She moves away from Hobbies and
    Sways over to the Fiction
And chooses a pretty title, like
    'The Rosy Crucifixion'. . . .
There's the acned youth who, against the odds,
    Kneels before the stock
Of Hegel, Kant and Schopenhauer,
    Kierkegaard and Locke.
The assistant smiles and turns to arrange
    The Historical Biography;
As soon as she does, he's up and across
    To the Nude and Glamour Photography.
There's the sandalled, shorted, bearded type
    With odorous rucksack,
Who unfolds all the Ordnance Survey maps
    And then can't fold them back.
There's the vicar who, all innocence
    In his suit of black and white,
Asks for another Trollope
    To take to bed at night.
Or the man who wants a book about
    'That fellow . . . ahh . . . you know—
It's called the . . . something something;
    Came out a while ago.'
And the author's name? He's not quite sure;
    Begins with G or O.
There are some who duck beneath the guard
    With a straight request or two,
Then want to know if Dr Johnson's
    Published something new.

And how to describe those saintly ones
　　Who deal with them each day?
Perhaps we'd best imagine what
　　A dealer's list would say:
Loose-hinged and just a little worn
　　But unfoxed—in clean DJ.

A Traditional Easter
or
Isn't it Martyrdom Enough Having to Deal with Tax Returns without Having to Enjoy Yourself with the Family?

Traditions in plenty can be found
At Easter: the sweet, spiced smells
Of hot-cross buns; pale, morning suns
That tumble between church bells;

While over the misted vicarage lawn
Where faithful feet have trod,
The church–appeal thermometer points,
With Gothic grace, to God.

Blackbirds in beeches sing Messiaen
With effortless cantilena,
While local choirs crucify
Handel, Bach and Stainer.

There's Toblerone on the telephone,
The books are veneered with bon-bon,
And down in the hall on a pristine wall
There's *Such*ard work going on. . . .

There's chocolate on pyjama fronts,
There's chocolate down the chairs;
After Eights melt on breakfast plates,
And Smarties crunch on stairs.

It's chocolate that's responsible for
The baby's greenish hue
And the piano's F♯ above middle C
That strikes with a soggy 'thwh'.

There are other traditions, of course, like 'Hot-
Cross Motors'—an Easter game
Which we've probably all taken part in
But never given a name:

The government steals bits of carriageway,
Blocks the road with JCBs,
And it seems by the map that the only way back
Is via the Pyrenees;

So you drum your fingers and bite your nails
And smoulder in single file,
While the cars stretch out before and behind
For mile after metal mile.

The fun of the game is trying to get home
On almost invisible roads;
Or seeing how long you can last before
Your car or your bladder explodes.

Then there's 'Vegetarian Vandalism'—
A game for those middle classes
Who'd otherwise spend their time being real:
Singing folk-songs or rubbing brasses.

You take a trowel and rucksack
And stride off into the hills
And rip up bluebells, primroses, cowslips,
Anemones, daffodils,

To make a natural garden
For the natural Barratt homestead.
The point of the game is to stay out so long
That when you get home they're all dead.

And if you can leave some gates open wide,
Trample crops—extra pleasure's incurred:
The farmers can all play Easter games too!
'Lose a Living' or 'Hunt the Herd'.

There's another tradition—'Druid's Drape',
An age-old Easter ritual;
Nobody's sure what its origins are
But the practice is wide and habitual.

You take your possessions out of doors
And cast them to the winds;
It sets you free, symbolically,
From everything—Coke tins,

Greaseproof paper, bottles, tissues,
Cigarette packets, tea-leaves:
They lie and fester in the grass
Or wrap themselves round trees.

They'll be quite safe in their resting-place—
The British like fair play:
They'll pass and pass, and pass again
And they'll never take them away.

But Easter's a time for sacrifice,
To give in to another's view,
So everyone finishes up by doing
What nobody wants to do—

The Family Outing in the car
To the country house or park;
It starts with pouts and ends with bouts
Of vomiting in the dark.

But look what spring has brought to light
As you sulk along the way:
Brightly coloured walls that bloom
With SALFORD SKINS OK!

And on the river, among the reeds,
Sometimes you can see
A silvery gleam at the edge of the stream—
That's Trolli Sainsburii.

There's Lorryspill, Fool's Coil, Lady's Shift,
Dry Dipstick and Old Man's Crossbar;
And, shyly peeping from the ditch,
Toyota Rustica.

So, though the money that you spent
On ice-cream, sweets and rides
Must be spent again to remove the stain
Made by small but determined insides,

Remember the finest tradition's to come,
Not horrendous, not boring, not risky—
Perhaps more medicinal than truly traditional:
The bedtime treble whisky.

Grandmother's Footsteps

Grannies are mightier than pen or sword,
Stranger than fiction,
The best of both worlds and the found Lost Chord.

Grannies are the one good deed
In a naughty world;
The ultimate panacea, the friend in need.

Grannies are those blessed ones
Who buy you things
You shouldn't have—like trumpets, caps and guns.

Grannies are cooks of a nobler breed
Than mothers or school;
Wouldn't give house-room to cheese flan or swede.

Grannies exist to talk or play
Or listen to riddles:
Grannies are Christmas Eve—but every day.

Grannies have kitchen scales for treats,
Games, button-boxes
And scratched tins with their treasure trove of sweets.

They'll trust you in a room alone
With knick-knacks,
With records and the wind-up gramophone.

A tumbledown room with dusty nooks,
Old snapshots, postcards
And sage-green four-leafed clovers pressed in books;

And sepia sons with serious jaws
And pensive eyes,
As if they heard some far, deserved applause.

That's Granny, in youth, with bob and bangles;
Elfin, beautiful,
Wearing her innocence at rakish angles.

Her garden has apple tree and swing;
It's wild, untilled,
But bulbs rise like thermometers each spring.

It's desert, jungle or Khyber Pass
Or ocean waste
Where insects leap like bow-waves in the grass.

Her shed's a kingdom, quite forgotten
Where spiders scowl
And crane-flies hang from legs like crooked cotton.

But it's a cobwebbed paradise
Of clotted clockwork,
Of tins and toys and trivia and woodlice.

Grannies give you chocolate spread,
New long trousers
And an icy, stone-hot-water-bottled bed.

And every bedtime, after prayers,
Her draughty candle
Pulls mad elastic shadows down the stairs,

Leaving the hollow chimney sighs,
The awful owls,
The distant, lowing farm for lullabies.

Grannies have books you long to see:
Peter Pan,
Andersen, Rackham, yards of Arthur Mee;

And all along the living room,
That brown and gold
Didactic, stern, encyclopaedic gloom.

In annuals with purring pages
Thick as blankets,
Are stories your father read in the Middle Ages.

Grannies are mothers to the power 15:
Warm, wise,
Always the same, but never mere routine.

Grannies can't be bribed or bored;
Above all that.
Grannies, like Virtue, are their own reward.

And when, at university,
They say 'Discuss
The difference between prose and poetry',

It's not hard: every grandchild knows—
Though critics don't—
Grannies are poetry; parents merely prose.

Festival Overture

At Festival time in Britain
The long summer evenings pass
With recital, cantata, concerto, sonata
And many a Masterclass.

The sponsorship scheme has worked like a dream;
Ticket prices shouldn't trouble you:
You can get to every single event
For the price of a BMW.

As the long light falls on city walls
And the sky fades through yellow to peach,
Dinner-jacketed men will leaf
Through programmes at eight quid each;

And ladies will sip ice-cold champagne
And nibble their canapés
While The London Brass from the Guildhall grass
Waft a cool Renaissance blaze.

There are organ recitals and candlelit choirs,
There's Son et Lumière;
Predictably, and expensively,
There's opera everywhere:

Opera covered in pocket-fluff,
Opera stilted and still,
Or full of Significant Juxtapositions
Having been through the Jonathan mill.

And then there's the great, the world-famous tenor
Who was booked to make the thing go,
But he fails to turn up and we have to make do
With Placebo Domingo. . . .

Those hack reporters who've never learned
To read, let alone to write,
Fresh from beauty-contests, sport
And 'Council Raps Building Site',

Turn music critic for a month,
But keep the same perspective,
And sum up 'Figaro', 'Wozzeck' and Wagner
with 'Simple, but *so* effective. . . .'

But what a rich variety
These summer festivals bring:
All the best of those who play,
Conduct, compose or sing.

In Bath you can hear The Borodin Trio,
King's Singers, Vienna Boys' Choir,
The Academy of St Martin-in-
The-Fields, and Murray Perahia;

While, at Oxford, there's The Borodin Trio,
King's Singers, Vienna Boys' Choir,
The Academy of St Martin-in-
The-Fields, and Murray Perahia. . . .

No, there isn't much exciting, new;
The director has his reasons—
He knows he'll make a bob or two
If he *keeps* doing *The Four Seasons*.

Give the public what they like,
The safe, the solid, the stock:
Mozart, Brahms and Beethoven
And Vivaldi's punk baroque.

Directors, perhaps, think Festival-goers
Are anatomical wrecks
Who stand on their dignity, pay through the nose
And talk through the back of their necks.

But let's not be too critical,
Let's not carp and whinge;
Of course, we have an alternative now—
Every Festival's grown a fringe

Where concerts are priced more reasonably,
There are more exciting ventures;
More real, more rough, more cultural—
And so much more pretentious.

There's the Peking Kabuki's version of
The Mousetrap—that's essential;
So is the exhibition of blank
Canvases, called 'Potential'.

Daley Thompson and Angela Rippon
Star in *Le Cid* on ice;
There's the Russian *Northanger Abbey*
And a play about two woodlice.

There's a musical based on the 'Gormenghast' books
Entitled *Peake-a-Boo!*
With AJ Ayer, Madonna, John Gielgud
And a holographed Irish stew.

John Cage will be playing all the rests
In the piano works of Liszt
On Liszt's *very own* piano—wow!
That's something not to be missed.

Marcel Marceau is miming the whole
Of the novels of Walter Scott
In a forty foot bowl of custard, dressed
As the Lady of Shalott,

While Pat Cash reads *Das Kapital*
In Latin and Langue d'Oc
Accompanied by Stockhausen's *Gruppen*
Arranged for harmonium and wok,

At the same time as topless gymnasts pose
As items from Yellow Pages
In a model of Gandhi's digestive tract
Made of shoe-trees and parrot-cages.

Yes, the Festival season is here again
With culture for the mass;
Let's welcome the deadly, the dismal, the dull
The chronic and the crass.

Envoi
or
Just a Thought. . . .

Remember, too, that at Festival time
Mr Lawson chuckles with glee—
Thinking of all that wealth of Art?
No, just the VAT.

There's something neat in using the talent
Of Rostropovich, say,
To provide the money for one missile more
To blow his homeland away.

Thirty-nine Winks

Oh sleep, it is a gentle thing
Beloved from Pole to Pole,
From Spaniard to Spaniard, Greek to Greek,
But in Britain, on the whole,
We don't do that sort of thing.

Some races pull sombreros down
Over puffed, post-prandial eyes
As a safety net for sunlight and
An aerodrome for flies,
But hardly in Walton-on-Thames.

No, the heat in Chipping Norton,
Bawtry, Cockermouth or Cheam
Is not enough to warrant stopping
Work to lie and steam,
So what would be the point?

In Britain, too, we seldom spend
Our nights like other nations—
Frittering time outdoors with wine
And long, deep conversations;
Good gracious me, no.

Our evenings are sacrosanct
To cultural fiestas:
EastEnders, Wogan, Dynasty—
That's when we need siestas.
So it's all quite sensible, really.

Salt of the Earth

Come, all ye lubbers, and oak-hearted men,
The Boat Show showboat is afloat again;
Prepare for salty and seafaring tales
Of Earl's Court and its January sails.
It's scarcely opened: they've already had
The dull, the daft, the stinking rich, the mad:
The public in its rich variety;
Yet each a convert *and* a missionary,
And all agog to seek the deep, blue yonder
By courtesy of fibreglass and Honda.
This is the time when every decent chap
Who knows a bilge-pump from a kicking strap
Can probe, inspect, compare each shining yard
Of raft or floating palace—no holds barred!
You can see him coming half a mile away,
Self-conscious in sea-going disarray:
The new brushed denim, trainers and blue cotton
Shirt, a natty cap—he's got the lot on;
Or perhaps a curly pipe and woolly hat—
The armchair yachtsman, essence of anorak,
Come for his yearly trip to hull and back.
Upholding the Condor and St Bruno image,
But adrift in Earl's Court and at sea in Greenwich.
With hip flask, guernsey, the current 'Cape Horner' mag,
And a battered Penguin Conrad in his bag.
He's got the jargon at his fingertips;
Not for him those telling verbal slips
That neophytes might make; knows boats from ships,
Port from starboard—but still has a dread
(Macbeth-like) of making the green one red.

He's not exactly Nelson's born successor:
A window-shopper, and a window-dresser.
He hails from Harlow, Milton Keynes or Penge
And owns an eight-foot rowboat—called *Revenge*. . . .
He toasts his cronies with a bluff 'chin-chin!'
And downs his loathed (but de rigueur) pink gin.
His house is named—well, you've already guessed:
'Spinnakers', 'Genoa', 'Lee Shore' or 'Crow's Nest'.
His wildest dream is captaining a clipper;
His dearest, a barman who will call him 'Skipper'.
He scorns, of course, what he calls 'rich men's toys'—
The fast, sleek, dieseled, seagoing Anglepoise;
For him there's nothing sweeter than the noise
Of wind in halyards, foam ripped up awry,
The long unpainted canvas of the sky
Or bristle of rain, the crack as mainsheets belly—
Especially when *he's* at home and *it's* on telly.
He's not a Richard Branson or Ted Heath
But owns, he's sure, their qualities. Underneath.
He's got the know-how, grit, ambition, dash:
The only thing that stops him's lack of cash.
He, faced with a smooth, expensive racing yacht
And a smooth, expansive salesman, coughs a lot,
Blushes a bit and ends up by admitting
That the ones he's got at Fishbourne need refitting;
And hopes, by that, the salesman will infer
That those in Poole are far superior.
He admires her cockpit, praises her graceful curves,
Is impressed by her draft and, really, he deserves
An Oscar for his grudging nod and 'Nice!',
And the way he seems half-tempted at that price,
And goes 'to think about it' over tea—
Which leaves him in the black by 14p.

He's learned a lot; perhaps the paramount—
The clean lines of a good expense account.
And for a week or two when he gets back,
He'll kick and curse his little fishing smack,
Barnacled, blistered, otiose and poor;
But, come the summer, he'll love her as before,
Knowing full well he never could relax
On forty snow-white feet of fiddled tax.

Voices from Grub Street

The English-speaking poets were obsessed
By food. I don't suppose you've noticed that:
It's not a thing most readers would have guessed,
But go into the study, shift the cat,
Sit down and start to write on food yourself
And ghosts of writers long since dead will rise,
And trip in solemn congress from the shelf
To gaze upon your work with hungry eyes.

I could have asked them for a line to quote:
I didn't; I said '*You* write,—and they wrote:

First, Emily Dickinson who fancied Chinese.

> I knew my Self concealed—a joy—
> The day—a Festival!
> Could I but make—Discovery—
> Something—Comestible.
>
> Seeking—tired—to dispel
> The ache—within this Clay—
> I slowly passed—identified—
> The Chinese take-away.
>
> One took my coin—inscrutably—
> For prawns and rice—but then—
> Invisibly—an hour passed—
> I longed to eat—again.
>
> My deed already done—entombed—
> With Life's indemnities—
> One Choice—to change—and I would take—
> Fish—chips—and mushy peas.

Then A E Housman who had a sandwich in a Shropshire field.

> Oh, all the fields are green, lad,
>   And all the welkin's blue;
> And half a hundred summers
>   Seem eating here with you.
>
> The cows are in the pasture,
>   The matins bell has rung
> Down where Dick would drive them
>   When he was twelve years young.
>
> Though Dick has grown a man, now,
>   He still sleeps out of doors;
> And he has in his wooden box
>   A harder cheese than yours.
>
> So lie you there and munch, lad,
>   The summer soon is fled;
> And time enough for being munched
>   When you and youth are dead.

And Robert Browning who tried Luigi's Trattoria.

This table? Good, then let's sit down. I was saying. . . .
Bah! Tush! And the sun as hot as it was that day
In Firenze (th' word's Italian: 'Florence' you'd say).
What did I wear my raincoat for? Or why
Did I wear it; take your choice—the grammar's a detail
Concerns not me. Food, d'you say? Ah, yes!
A reminder—to my argument. What's for lunch?
The bush, though metaphoric's had its beating,
For one of my failures is to interrupt
And, like as not, to show my erudition
With reference, here and there, to Ghirlandaio
Or, less obscure, Fra Whatsisname and Titian;

Thus making my verse half rich, Handelian chorus,
And half Victorian, vernacular Thesaurus.
So—no more interlarded exclamations;
They can become a habit. Grrr! Begone!
So, there! Well . . . hmmmmm, now—yes, ahem! Where
  was I?
Let's see the menu. What's this? Hamelin Soup?
I had it once, with Snail Upon the Thorn—
Escargots à la Pippa—well garni,
That a chef from Innsbruck casseroled for me;
I belched, you belched, he belched, we belched all three.
Next, Osso Bucco—wasn't he the man
Who did the frescoes in the Pitti Palace?
Lasagne, ravioli, tortellini. . . .
Pasta! Enough! (You get the pun, I hope?
I don't do this for fun, but reputation.)
And coffee with After Eights. . . . No, not today;
But chocolate, yes: Roses, Roses, all the way.
Perhaps we'll have . . . Oh, dear, the sentence ends
Without an object. So what? There's a motto:
Non omnia possumus omnes salves the conscience.
Retournons à nos moutons—that's advice
To me as well as you, for food et cetera
Is not my forte—foreign word again!
But that's all one: I can take my leave in four—
Adieu, farewell, vale, arrivederci!

Psummer Psalm

1 In weariness will I lift up mine head: and my voice in supplication.
2 Stop not thine ears to my lamentation: but consider my complaint.
3 For hath it not been stablished of old: that the twenty-first of June is the beginning of summer?
4 Since also the twenty-fourth thereof is Midsummer's Day, it taketh not a mathematical genius, ño, nor a second Einstein, to work out: that the whole thing is over in seven days.
5 'Great!' saith man, 'Oh, great! Yea, exceeding great!: I mean, wherein lieth the point?
6 For LO! we have scarcely got round to cutting back the clematis, to oiling the lawnmower, melting last year's Christmas tree lights off the plant propagator and unwrapping the *Observer*-offer patio sun-lounger available in three exciting shades: and, behold, the nights are drawing in!'
7 Here cometh the weather forecast: and here is Ian MacGaskill, that Leviathan whom thou hast made to take his pastime therein.
8 He riseth and speaketh abominations: storm and tempest fulfilling his word.
9 Is man a duck that THOU rainest over him: that thou turnest the garden into an mighty flood?
10 LO! There go the cuttings from the brother-in-law's geraniums: the antirrhinums, the trailing lobelia, the little red things with a funny name, what is it again, and the bedding plants at seventy pee a punnet which THOU hast made.
11 Yea, test matches are rained off also: and Wimbledon shall make its usual splash.

12 Johnston, Blofeld and Martin-Jeńkins shall gnash their teeth: Maskell and Williams shall bring forth winds and vapours.

13 How long will the tribes of Benidorm and Torremolinos mock me and revile me?: they show forth their tans, they wag their heads and shoot forth their lips saying 'Where is now thy summer?'

14 When shall I stand in thy courts, O Butlins: or who shall be found in the porches of the Royal Esplanade Hotel, Corporation St, Clacton CL3 7GS?

15 For the sea-wind gnaweth as with teeth of glass: who shall withstand his hailstorms?

16 Even he that hath long-johns and plastic raiment: though the noontide be dark under his feet.

17 Bognor Regis is my washpot: over Skegness will I cast my shoe.

18 Yet will I sing of mercy and loving-kindness: for I suppose THOU hast, at least, given man bus-shelters for a refuge.

19 Therein may he eat his fish and chips, yea, his mushy peas also: while lolly-papers, crisp-packets, Coke cans, Kleenex, Kentucky Fried Chicken boxes and non-biodegradable polythene bags wrap about his rain-soaked ankles.

20 Summer cometh and he saith 'Tush': yea, Tush shall be ever upon his lips.

Amen

Birthday Ode
to the Poet's Daughter

Because
Of all the usual things
I love you.
Because
Of your innocent sabotage
Of sewing-machine
Or cat.
Because
You run, smile, laugh
At me,
At rain.
Because
You are (of course)
Beautiful.
Because
You talk so much
Without pretending,
Because
You love without pretending;
But most of all
Because
Of the ambitious
Size
Of your
Boots.

Fifteen Ways of Looking at a Duck

Redshanks, thin as their whistles, flake
The estuaries
Where flat, grey seas fidget, fold and break.

They gather in anthologies,
While the bullfinch,
Football shirted, mugs the invisible breeze.

The wagtail twirls his moustaches,
Dinner-jacketed,
Looking high and low for his galoshes;

And the owl, the owl spins the wise
Round world
Along the axis of his dinner-plate eyes.

But ducks don't fit the avian mould;
Jesters. Urchins.
A kind of bird, that won't be what it's told.

They move like matrons on the land,
With heavy bags
Clutched in each imaginary hand.

Or dibble in a puddle's shallows,
Frowning;
Fat and firm and fluffy, like marshmallows.

Ducks swimming comfortably make
Slow symmetries;
A Rorschach pattern on a page of lake.

They whisper on the waterway—
Ripples, rustles,
Like the soft sound of deer running away.

They wobble and tack round willow-fronds,
Busy, important,
Like dirty tugs between the Cunard swans.

They thrash the water white for bread;
There's always one
Who grabs the best, and one who's never fed.

They speak sandpaper language; glottal;
A corkscrew loudly
Failing to screw a cork out of a bottle.

Enamelled faces continually check,
And are surprised by,
Legs, like a lizard's or a dowager's neck.

Ducklings disappoint their mother;
Just another duck—
Spoon at one end, feather-duster at the other.

Ducks put their heads on backwards when
They roost;
As if they'd turn back into eggs again.

V's and W's melt and pass
Where distant ducks
Score the pond like diamond on glass.

They're a splash of colour in winter fog
Which, elsewhere,
Scribbles only a monochrome, passing dog.

If one dislimns in the thickening air,
The rest wink;
Make jokes about the mallard imaginaire.

Three, at evening, flying high,
Turn to brass ducks,
Pinned by sunset to the suburban sky.

And These Come Interest-Free . . .

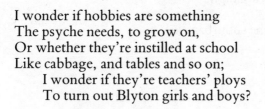

What are the British famous for?
Well—Tower Bridge, of course;
Beer, C of E, democracy,
The house, the hat, the horse,
    Nelson's column, London Bobbies
    But, most of all, for having hobbies.

I wonder if hobbies are something
The psyche needs, to grow on,
Or whether they're instilled at school
Like cabbage, and tables and so on;
    I wonder if they're teachers' ploys
    To turn out Blyton girls and boys?

They're always set as essays
For young examinees;
They appear in theatre programmes,
On book jackets, in CVs;
    You're a dullard if you don't spot trains,
    Grow orchids, paint, build model planes.

No other nation takes the same
Abiding, deep delight
In how the famous spend their time
When they are out of sight.
    Don't other nations work at what
    They have to, but would rather not?

The British, though, refuse to mix
Their businesses with pleasure;
They hide their real selves when at work
And bring them out at leisure;
  If you want to see the British 'live'
  Then watch them after half past five.

They stream from their commuter trains
And into their Volvo estates,
Athirst to dig, to feed the pig,
Or decorate their plates,
  Or print their photos (large amounts
  Of Sue and Tricia in Accounts).

Crafty shops are flooded with
Incompetent enquiries
Spawned from reading certain Edwardian
Ladies' Country Diaries;
  While housewives sew their ropey sandals,
  Architects make listed candles.

Bank managers play string quartets,
Musicians plant and weed,
Landscape gardeners go on stage
And actors go to seed;
  They all find ease and peace of mind
  In someone else's daily grind.

I can't think why they didn't get
A job to suit their pleasure,
To give them satisfaction
Plus a salary for good measure;
  But then, the grass is always greener
  Once outside the main arena.

I wonder, though, in what pastimes
The well-known find enjoyment?
And whether they contrast with or
Reflect their true employment?
    We can't be certain what they do—
    But one could have a guess or two:

Keith Best, MP for Anglesea,
Is learning to count and read;
He's having six lessons at a time
But they don't think he'll succeed.
    Estate Agents have fun enough—
    Their hobby's playing 'Call My Bluff'.

John Motson is a stereo freak,
(That's 'types' rather than 'phonic');
Customs and Excise men play 'Strip
Jack Naked' for their tonic;
    The *Sun* gives voyeur-training free:
    Their Hobbies Column's on page three.

Terry Wogan's hobby's astronomy—
He loves stars. Magnifies them.
Thus proving they are mostly gas
Once you analyse them.
    The hobby of Oliver Reed affords
    Impersonations of newts and Lords.

And I just have fun with my *Teach Yourself Thermo-*
    Nuclear Devices,
Or plastering cities with 'No Through Road'
    And spitting in tourists' ices.
    Fun? Well, yes; but a change, above all
    From throwing myself at the padded wall.

Grace Abounding

for the launching of the *Grace O'Malley*
named after the famous Elizabethan pirate

An awkward Grace, you are, in limbo
Of dry land now;
Your easy lines landlubbered and akimbo.

Tied, yourself, to England's leg
While beneath you the sea
Rucks and wrinkles on its restless bed

And all your fabled piracies
Dormant; shrunk
To plunder and pillage of the local breeze.

Shivering in the wind, you feel
The world's drag,
The wide and soundless tons beneath your keel;

Waiting for water's ropes to bite
And your wake curdle,
Frosting the green with parallels of white.

Your sails will sing and taut sheets spell
White descants
Over the rich groundbass of the swell;

Free as shearwaters are free
To swing and dip
In the shape of the big wind's unshaped melody.

But how will you treat the Hoo-ray set,
Grace O'Malley?
The acned anoraks? The chinless wet?

The topless teens, the ghetto-blasters?
Boozed crews?
The nonchalant, navigational near-disasters?

Oh, Grace, how your bow-wave curls
In a green sneer
At crass captains, at fluffy Tiller girls,

And simpering sloops that buck and slide
Giggling, on
The teasing slap and tickle of the tide.

Silently, you'll add to silence
Shadows of sound,
Watercoloured diphthongs, soft beguilements;

Your hull slippery with reflections
Of the waves' cobbles
That nudge you to your courteous genuflections.

And off the shoulder of the night
You'll lean at evening,
Snagged in the nets and honeycombs of light.

Echo, Grace, the hue and sigh
Of long noons;
Of chalky gulls on the scratched, blue slate of sky;

Or, rocking at anchor by blowsy bars,
All night long,
Your masthead tracing circles through the stars.

Or struggling uphill with wind awry,
Rip the foam
From the sea's roots and swipe it to the sky.

Piratical and priestlike tasks:
Be and know
The answers to the questions water asks;

Your clean, applied geometry
Smooth and solve
The slopings and the stratagems of sea.

Be, Grace, in your element;
Never tame
But tamed, complaisant, captive by consent.

Go, Grace, amid the gathering calms;
Go, Grace—
Run safely to the green world's open arms.

Rustle of Spring

The winter's rains and ruins are over,
The world's out of quarantine.
March: the old earth bestirs itself,
The first signs of spring can be seen
Where Estate Agent's notices shyly peep
Black and white through the burgeoning green.

I'm afraid it's time for gardening again,
Though the garden's a muddy sea
Where bare-branched shrub and newly hatched grub
Exist precariously
In a symbiotic balance with
Detritus Dustmanii.

You can go by the gardening books, of course,
But you'll find that your work load doubles;
I'm the man to steer you past
Those horticultural troubles:
The man who thought hardy annuals
Were *Jude the Obscure* with bubbles.

There are things the gardening books don't say
And which take some time to dawn;
Such as, grass—when it grows in flowerbeds—
Is like thistle and nightshade and thorn,
An extremely hardy perennial; but
It's an annual in a lawn.

The lawn, by the way, is that rough, brown patch
Like a seashore at low tide,
Or a cross between an old doormat
And a moulting camel-hide.
It's very fond of children, though;
It follows them inside.

Now, if you're a serious gardener
Your shed will boast at least
50 per cent of the following:
One bicycle (deceased),
An axe-head, a trowel, a hamster cage
And a map of the Middle East;

Six 1940s *Radio Times*
And a programme from Scofield's *Lear*,
A small dismay in macramé,
Half a kit for making beer,
Nineteen fags and some extra-strong mints
Left over from Lent last year;

A coil of rope without an end,
A hose without a spout,
A biscuit tin with one screw in,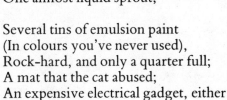
Some shears, with one screw out;
Four Scrabble tiles, two rusting files,
One almost liquid sprout;

Several tins of emulsion paint
(In colours you've never used),
Rock-hard, and only a quarter full;
A mat that the cat abused;
An expensive electrical gadget, either
Incomplete or fused.

Now some Gardening Hints: grow dahlias—
They always delight the eyes.
They don't look much when you plant them first—
They're a nondescript colour and size—
But in summer . . .! They turn to soggy, brown sticks
Covered with little green flies.

You can't grow asters to match the ones
On the packet; don't even hope to—
'A blaze to remember from June to November!'
Believe that? Well, you'd be a dope to;
And the heliotrope, like a damp bit of rope—
There's no helio for it to trope to!

If you'd like to combine your gardening
With local history,
Just build a blazing bonfire out of
Last year's Christmas tree
And a neighbour will quote you each by-law made
Since 1763.

And those corms you wrapped in newsprint and
Packed carefully on a tray,
And kept in an even temperature
Away from the light of day—
Now's the time to bring them out
And throw them all away.

The seedlings you spent a fortune on
Last week at the nursery,
Should be planted out in semi-shade
Nine inches apart—not three—
So the cat can destroy them one by one
Whenever it has a pee.

And what gardening manuals will never explain
Is rules Nos 1 and 2:
Wherever you dig there's a layer of rock
Impossible to get through;
Whatever you've done by the end of the day
Dogs and children will always *un*do.

Oh, you'll blister and bruise and get broken nails,
Your back will be sore and bennt;
But when your garden's finished, at last,
You'll not grudge the effort you've spent.
I'm giving mine its top-dressing today:
I've ordered the sand and cement. . . .

It's a Well Known Fact That. . . .

The Greeks had a word for it—Democracy,
Which, loosely translated, these days, means Hypocrisy.
Democracy: a political expedient
To keep a government more or less obedient,
Has changed its flavour, sucked dry by a nation
Lacking in logic, thought and application;
What used to be a safety-valve for fairness
Is now an excuse for massive unawareness.
'Equal in worth' means 'IQ just as high?'
At best a falsehood and at worst a lie;
And only he whose brain is flour-and-paste
Can generalize about such things as taste.
But, to the dull, the word has always been
A war-cry—viz. like us, small, bland and mean,
Bringing on slow, but sure, deterioration
As comprehensive as an education
Where teachers rather choose to be defeatist
Than risk the awful epithet 'élitist',
Which means to enter classrooms knowing more
Than little Willie Watkins in G4.
So children fit for Coleridge or Blake
Have to refrain for their coevals' sake;
Innocence and Experience are all one
While they spell out 'See, Peter, see me run!'
For none must grow up in the heresy
That others are more skilled than he or she;
And better be unfit, bored, on the booze
Than play team games where one side has to lose,
For losing might bring on some awful trauma—
Perhaps we're all skilled, but different! Getting warmer. . . .

What gardener, seeing some plants red, some blue,
Would dye them both some pallid, neutral hue
Or paint them all red, shouting 'Blue is vanity!'
A kind of horticultural insanity;
And yet it happens to us every hour
When clichés are allowed the slogan's power.
It's only snobs who listen to Radio 3—
They must learn the taste of the majority;
And Mrs Whitehouses—hung up on sex—
Prevent Detectives singing on our sets.
Whatever you would like to hear, do, see,
Must still be measured by the LCD.
Because I couldn't take a test-match wicket
Should we stop Ian Botham playing cricket?
And I, of course, should not write poetry:
Well, Ian's not got my vocabulary.
Few can match the technique of Oistrakh:
We'll stop that blighter playing Brahms and Bach.
And Jacobi's Hamlet, and his Cyrano—
Amazing! Well, the man will have to go.
We'd soon lack interest, comfort and facilities
Were the world tailored to my capabilities;
And sows' ears wouldn't make a silken purse
Were the standard yours, or his, or hers.
Do we democratize our private lives
And ask for votes when choosing husbands, wives?
We don't take referenda in the street
When tea time comes, on what we ought to eat,
Nor take advice from MPs in a hurry,
Or every night we'd have Edwina curry.

It's only, I'm afraid, disparity
That allows courage, generosity,
Art itself, humour, love, self-sacrifice
And all the other things we claim to prize;
And how can any world be really free
When modes of freedom are compulsory?
Before we go too mad I'd like to know
Who says of anything 'It Shall Be So'?
'The majority of Citizens like this best—
We'll thrust it, willy-nilly, on the rest'.
And how do they know the majority like x
From random samples of average age and sex?

I wonder why there shouldn't come a time
When being quiet, for instance, was a crime.
And all the hours of silence that I savour
Provoke an angry protest from my neighbour.
Must I sit up and watch all-night TV
Because he likes to be disturbed at three,
Or hold wild parties to breed shrieks and screams
Because he can't bear silence and sweet dreams?
You think I've gone too far? Well, maybe so:
But be on guard, or that's the way we'll go.
The laws of arithmetic limp to the wall:
Small mind plus small mind makes mind-twice-as-small
And universal darkness covers all.

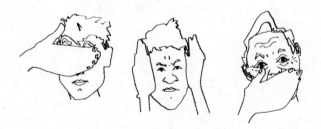

The Village Fête

A morning, fresh from the wrong side of the bed,
Whacks wind with more wind, tips the clouds about,
Rips meaning from a shout;
Pulls down the rain
And sulks behind it.

There's a damp despondency, at eight,
About the village fête. But then, at nine,
A sudden yawn of sunlight breaks
And the green smells like wine,
Sprouts trestle-tables, vans, rock cakes;
And chutney-bearing matrons come
Like ducks in a wobbling line.

The hired marquees,
Folded like giant's handkerchieves,
Jolt behind dung-dishevelled tractors
Which score a zig-zag frown
Into the grass,
Making the green one brown.

'Testing, testing; one, two, one, two,'—
Mr Molineux,
Running the PA like a dog with a bone.
He wires up, haphazardly, the school gramophone
And scratches out Sullivan overtures,
Black Lace, Massed Bands, Acker Bilk.
The air above the tea-urns blurs
And shakes, like watered silk.

The bookstall's full of *Woman's Realm*
Outdated economic theories,
Thick, clean paperbacks
Branded 'Now a Major TV Series!'
And still unsuited
To those who like their English Lit diluted.

There's *Common Sense in Compost Making,*
Wartime Baking,
One battered J M Barrie, Charles Reade, Gissing;
Two Agatha Christies with the last page missing.
The vicar's pocketed *Emmanuelle III,*
Mistaking it for Bible commentary.

At two o'clock, an actor of small fame,
(Once seen for thirty seconds on TV
In *Hi-de-Hi* and a pilot panel-game),
Steals some showbiz stories from *Dear Me,*
Pretends they're his, drops the odd big name
Into the PA — which fails,
Squirts nothing but decibels;
Sounds like someone
Sandpapering a school of whales.

Tent-flaps flog the wind
With a sound like stage thunder;
Children are slapped for crawling under.

Dogs, raffish, debonair,
Trace the longest distance between
Over there and over there
And check it again and again.

Men with lists on clipboards
Ticked and crossed,
Search for something that they haven't lost.

Already there's a fifteen minute queue
For the tombola and the Portaloo;
Emma, aged six, wins the malt whisky
In the Treasure Hunt;
Her father gets the roll-on deodorant.

Grannies in black, roll by like baby grands;
Sister with tearful sister, holding hands.
Babies in prams, home-made jams;
Farmers in suits like tortoises in shells.
Coconut shyers, footballs through tyres,
Beer, crushed grass,
Hot-dog, gymkhana smells.

Miss Madeley is nervous of the weather;
Miss Johnson of green hair, motorbikes, black leather.

The fancy dress brings scarecrows, fairies, sheiks;
Dried ice-cream peels like gold-leaf from their cheeks.

At five, the draw: the raffle's won
By the organizer's son.
Miss E Banks wins the cured ham, for the quiz;
No one knows who Miss Banks is.
The chocolates go to Mrs Penn,
The pig to Mr Weekes — again.

Some desultory applause;
The populace, in twos and threes, withdraws
With heat-oppressed bunions,
Pushchairs filled with coconuts,
Cake-stands, annuals, pickled onions.

Village Venuses rise from the foam
Of cow parsley, meadow fescue,
Smooth their crumpled skirts and dawdle home.

Vital Statistics

I love that mad, statistical foray
Into wild fantasy, as when they say

That if all the custard that was consumed in the Home
Counties during the Second World War were gathered
together, it would be enough to cover a county as large as
Devon
To a depth of five feet seven.

I can't help thinking how
It would first bewilder, then wipe out, the cow.

Or,
If all the telephone directories in the whole of the world were
laid end to end, they would stretch seventeen times round
the Equator.

Many, of course, would get wet, or chewed
By romantically named and exotically hued
Sea creatures;
And what a terrible distance to go
To find a number in Herstmonceux
Or Bude.

If all, may I reply, the moles that ever tunnelled under this
field were to sneeze simultaneously, the resultant tremor
would be enough to send the entire string section of the
London Philharmonic Orchestra from the Festival Hall
dressing rooms into the Thames at a mean speed of eight
point five miles an hour.

Or
If all the breaths which ever said 'I love you'
Were exhaled again, at once, there might be wind
Enough to blow away the fragile reasons
For never having done so; certainly
Enough to send a rocketship to Mars
If not to Jupiter (the whole of which,
By the way, if dropped in the Atlantic,
Would float).

We'll Be Back
after the Break. . . .

There's an end-of-term feeling about July
That touches every creature.
In schools they stand to hear the grand
Farewells from the headteacher:
A cross between Kipling, McGonagall, Job
And the end of a *Lassie* feature.

Office typewriters are shrouded. TV
Series come to an end;
The dress shops are full of autumn fashions.
What does it all portend?
H-O-L-I-D-A-Y,
Pronounced 'Shove, sweat and spend'.

The car's been serviced, the timetables bought,
The plants all left in a row;
The windows are shut, the gas is off,
The milk's been stopped, and so
All that's left is those last-minute tasks
Like deciding where to go. . . .

Dumping the dog at the kennels, perhaps,
Is the hardest job of all,
For he gives you, as you leave him in
His bare, monastic stall,
A glance like Michael Parkinson
Looking at Lauren Bacall.

And then it's back to load the car
With dolls, pens, Thermos, shoes,
Maps, books, games, fruit, pills, creams, hat, flute,
Boots, mack, bulbs, jack, spare fuse
And all the thousand other things
You'll find you never use.

The children scream and play 'I-Spy',
The M1 traffic roars;
The radio is on full blast
But can't drown Granny's snores;
And mother's loud silence means 'Are the passports
Still on the chest of drawers?'

The airport car park is Sainsbury's
To the power of 33:
A do-it-yourself Disneyland
Of tarmac and draggled tree;
You cleverly start at car park M
And find a space in B.

And then it's all armpits and plastic macks
Thronging the duty-free;
Samsonite and expense accounts
As far as the eye can see;
And everyone looks as if they've been here
Since 1973.

Some passengers banish their nervousness
By pandering to the belly;
Some watch the indicator board
As avidly as the telly,
For flights not in, not out, not now,
And some not on your Nelly.

There's the school trip's decibelligerence,
An acned adrenalined row;
One teacher, bald, be-suited and
Responsible of brow;
And one all knees and anorak,
Gung-holier than thou.

For the price you paid, you didn't expect
The plane would be brand new,
But there's still the sinking of the heart
When, standing in the queue,
You notice the strips of elastoplast
On the door . . . of the outside loo.

From incoming flights leap homeward hordes
Like well-done toast from toasters,
With plastic toreador matchbox-holders,
Rioja and bullfight posters,
And already inventing stories of how
They made it with the hostess.

On board the steward begins his task
Of, so nonchalantly, relaying
Emergency procedures, that
You don't take in what he's saying,
Entranced by the stewards who stand and perform
What looks like aerobics or praying.

And thus begins a fortnight of
Enforced British urbanity
In the face of foreign food and customs
Bordering on insanity;
Two weeks to kill amid the shrill
Sad musak of humanity.

And all so that envious friends may hear
About poor old Sandra's insides,
And what that girl from Newcastle did
With every one of the guides;
And how it was 'this' when it should have been 'that'
—All backed up with foggy slides.

arrivals
DELAYED

Defending the Title

Whether you start with Adam and Eve
Or with Darwin, equality
Must surely have been a mark of Man
Since the dawn of History;
So where did we get this odd idea
Of aristocracy?

I'm afraid, if you look at the evidence,
There isn't a lot of room
For thinking anyone privileged;
So it started, we must assume,
From basic working-class values—viz.
Who can bash up whom?

These Lordlings in their castle keeps
(State-aided if not rented)
Not being genial and merry, like peasants,
Soon grew discontented.
This could have been the reason that
Serf-riding was invented.

But Oh! *Tempus edax rerum!*
What started as nobility
Sank, by degrees, through the centuries
To a mildewed, mild gentility,
And now is very little more
Than economic utility.

Still, the upper classes have given the world
Burke's Peerage, 400th edition,
And . . . something else—what was it now?
Safari Parks in Britain!
And look what they've done for literature—
Macaulay and Bulwer-Lytton. . . .

While the lower orders have only produced
Shakespeare, Johnson, Dickens,
Coleridge, Hardy, Newton, Pope,
All of our musicians,
Eliot, Pinter, Larkin, Joyce,
And some Royal Academicians,

Webster, Milton, Hopkins, Shaw,
Clare, Keats and Chesterton,
Wordsworth, Chaucer, de la Mare,
Perhaps not Xenophon,
But Dylan Thomas, Nesbit, Gray,
Blake, Browning, and Anon.

But before you nod in sage agreement,
Don't forget it's true
They've given us Little and Large, EastEnders,
And Mrs Thatcher, too;
And I doubt if Motson's or Coleman's blood
Is a *very* deep shade of blue.

But Englishmen from comprehensive
Or from Public Schools
Are not, thereby, more fortunate
Or even Fortune's fools;
Time was when Britain ruled the waves,
But now she waives the rules.

For time has a way of levelling
And fashions ebb and flow;
Do the hoi polloi say 'Lord bless you, sir!'
Or the gentry 'Doncherknow'?
The upper lip may still be stiff
But the abdomen's let go.

So everything's turned upside down
And the aristocracy
Are tied to keeping up stately homes
And providing buns and tea
Not for debs, but coachloads of plebs
From Dudley and Bexhill-on-Sea.

Contrariwise, the vocal Left
Who are all for title-shedding,
Perhaps sometimes feel there's something more real
Than pedestrian precincts in Reading,
And turn out in their millions
To watch a royal wedding.

Yes, the English are a funny lot;
Never quite sure what they mean,
But they've always regarded a title—
Duke, Earl, Lord, Viscount, Queen—
As tantamount to a halo: just
Another thing to clean.

Shapes of Childhood

A child: me, sitting in a wood.
I see him from here,
High on the abstract hill of adulthood.

He constructs me randomly
From what's at hand;
Careless of what I will or want to be.

Look what goes in: shapes, smells,
School-dinners,
Hymns, grazed knees, snow and ice-cream bells;

Log-light, rosemary, wallflower,
Cowsheds, paraffin lamps,
Rupert, the Psalms, E Nesbit, Children's Hour.

The shapeless, terrible dressing-gown,
The spare room
Where spiders scuttle like a moving frown.

Candle flame and conifer,
Wet tarmac;
Being, again, demoted from ink monitor.

All the living and the dead
Whisper syllables,
Pull lexicons about my singing head.

All seasons shall be sweet to me
Through his eyes,
His undulled ears, his quick complicity.

He stands beside the slab-still lake
Lidded with perspex,
Where leaves lie gummed and water boatmen skate.

In the warm bracken's corridors
Bees, grasshoppers
Trim the silence with their tiny saws.

Or at dusk on wakes of hay,
Smooth field-foam,
His three-foot shadow falls six feet away.

Moonlight, music, Christmas tree
He loves;
I watch him growing, growing helplessly.

In summer's late translucencies
He watches, stores
The tigerish colour twilight makes of trees;

Longs for autumn when the rain
Types exclamation marks,
Or scrawls italics on the window-pane,

And pewter skies drag on the hills:
Damp hammocks.
Mist translates to smoke which rucks and spills

Where the bonfire with a sharp crack
Sucks a vermilion eye
Into its cheek and drops a grey lid back.

December zips up the ditch;
Black hedges
Hem the field with immaculate tacking-stitch.

Or a morning frost makes sun splinter.
At the wood's edge
Trees exhale apprentice ghosts of winter.

I lean against infinity
This pile of selves:
Flotsam and jetsam, chance mythology.

A child: me, sitting in a wood.
He is me still,
Here on the abstract hill of adulthood.

Midweekendings

Bernard Matthews

Yes, Christmas is a funny time;
Part of it merely dutiful—
Bernard Matthews will try to provide
The bit that should be 'bootiful'.

But if you ruin your Christmas lunch
He won't give you any reduction:
*Bern*ard, don't forget, is his name
And not a cooking instruction.

Norman Willis

Norman Willis, painter, poet,
An artist in several media;
The next thing you know, we'll have Fischer-
    Dieskau
Singing Trades Union Lieder.

But the jargon he uses on 'Any Questions'
Or on 'Question Time'—
Can that be the linguistic basis
For a Norman Willis rhyme?

I hope not. Imagine if Shakespeare had been
A TUC jargon gent:
'At this moment in time is the winter
Of our discontent. . . .'

And he'd rewrite his best-known line,
'To be or not to be':
'A situation of aspiration
Or non-viability?'

George Mikes

He'll teach you anything you like
In language sesquipedalian:
How to be poor, a Guru, God,
Or how to be an alien.

His concept of the 'downstart' is
The one I like the best.
If you match it with the Guru
Do you get a Bud(dh)a Pest?

George set his foot on English soil
And must have been convinced:
He came here for a fortnight and
He's been here ever since;

Thus inheriting a homeland
As well as the one of his birth—
Blessed are the Mikes
For they shall inherit the earth. . . .

Michael Heseltine
MP

When you find a party's policies
More than a little alarming,
It's quite disturbing to discover
Its members rather charming.

I use that word advisedly—
It might be mentally harming
If I described Michael, or any other
Conservative, as 'disarming'. . . .

Marguerite Fawdry,
owner of
Pollocks Toy
Theatres

Ah, Pollocks! The splendid proscenium arch
In the gold of a bygone age
Contrasting (as in real theatre) with
The rubbish on the stage.

89

I mounted plays on a Pollock stage
When I was a tiny tot:
The poorest kind of theatre—
Not Grotowski so much as grot.

It did have side-effects: when
I first joined the rep at Stoke,
I thought you had to shuffle sideways
Every time you spoke. . . .

Dickie Bird

An attacking field for Dickie Bird:
Anne Robinson, lithe, assured;
John Duffield, short square Lego
And an extremely silly Forde.

Dickie's a harbinger of summer;
First sign that winter's gone—
Oh, the polished stump! The solid thump
Of leather on silly mid-on!

One yawn, one removal of the eye
From the ball or from the wicket'll
Ensure that whatever it was you missed
Will be absolutely cricketal.

Barry Tuckwell

Barry Tuckwell's career has given
St Paul the coup de grâce:
He can speak with love *and* the tongues of angels
And still be sounding brass.

There's a lot of mystique about the horn
(The orchestra's Lilith)
So it's very nice to meet the man
Behind the Hinde-myth. . . .

But beware the British Horn Festival:
A musically clammy day,
Listening to the semi-skilled
Playing *Semiramide*. . . .

Jane Glover

The trouble with coming as a woman
Into what's always reckoned
As a male preserve means sex
Comes first, and music second.

And the tabloids—peerless prizers
Of the noun-as-epithet—
May talk of men as 'Maestro' but
Jane Glover as 'Maestrette'.

Never mind the banalities
Of all the media cattle
And Karajan conducting till
Your Boults begin to Rattle.

Mel Calman is enough to make
An instant poet curse:
He can put as much into one small line
As would take a page of verse;

And is it just an accident
That 'mel' is Latin for honey?
Out of the strong came the sweetness,
And out of the tragic, the funny.

The little men that flow from his pen
With their innocent urbanity
Have struck a blow for socio-
Politically crushed humanity.

He's stamped his name on all our moods,
His style is so commodious:
He's Mel-ancholy, Mel-odramatic
But never, of course, Mel-odious.

Medici String
Quartet

Auctioning Beethoven String Quartets?
Well, it may bring the shekels in.
Next you'll be billed as 'Medici Trio—
Now with EXTRA violin!'

Or 'Who put the "Razz" into Razoumovsky?
The Medici did, oh yes!
Now hear their Janáček's "Intimate Letters"
With thrilling new PS.'

You'll know when sponsorship's gone too far
When they offer 50p
Off your next quartet whenever
You sit through Bartók 3.

Nicholas Coleridge What do Nicholas Coleridge
And Joe Orton share alone?
They've both produced a means for
Entertaining Mr Sloane.

Nicholas may be 'promising' but
The magazine's travelled far:
The *Queen* is now a co-regent and
Harpers, less bizarre.

Larry Gelbart How pleasant to meet Mr Gelbart
(If I may misquote Lear);
A funny thing happened on the way to his forum
And on the way to Korea;

He's perfectly caught the logical, manic
Official fatuity
That's supposed to keep Europe inviolate
In perpetuity.

And done it better than anyone
Has ever done it before;
Twice as well as some—in fact,
A sort of *Catch 44*.

Bob Champion I'd need the pen of Marlowe and
The lyric gift of Campion
If I were to do justice to
Our birthday guest, Bob Champion.

Bob joins a long line of those who hate
The newspaper graffiti,
Who go for the inessentials, not
The Ardonitty-gritty.

93

So here's to what will be, not what's been,
On or off the course;
For the future may you get nothing worse
Than just a little hoarse. . . .

Laurie Lee

He who thinks that life begins
When childhood's in the mist
Is as much like an adult as Harold Robbins
Is like a novelist.

If I may quote (and I often do:
It makes the verse more pleasant)
A happy birthday, Laurie Lee
'Now sit there for the present. . . .'

John Dankworth

Ther was among our merye entourage
A grete musician, somedele steeped in age
Who hadde stodied much in his musick
Biforn his moder bought a liquorice-stykke
And then to runne a bigge band, pardee,
That al had thoght impossibilitee!
John Dankworth—sixty yeres of razmatazz,
You see the rhyme approchynge? Wrong again
What other pleyer ranketh in his classe?
The sunne, I wys, it shyneth from his brasse.
Tho we ben both enamoured of grete sinnes,
For he loves sax and I love violins.

Julie Felix

Her idea of the healing power
Of music gets my vote,
And lends a whole new meaning to the
Phrase 'A Doctor's Note'.

Hi-Fi instead of high fibre?
(That's called the F♯ plan)
Broken arms are cured by Brahms
And croup by Crouperin;

A dose of tonic water music
Keeps the ague off;
Locke and Lawes will soothe your sores
And Rimsky Cures a cough. . . .

Roy Hattersley
MP

Roy Hattersley is interviewed
By the *Guardian*'s Jim Naughtie
And (since it's the *Guardian*) we may find
That he talks to Ron Hackersptree etaoin shrdl 4½.

Bishop of
Durham

Dr Jenkins has stirred up the Christian world—
Well, he must have expected some stones;
I suppose we could reduce *Don Giovanni*
To 'A conjuring trick with trombones'.

Prof Alan Peacock

Alan Peacock's our birthday guest,
Surrounded by BBC;
Why is he waving that big, white flag
And smiling so sheepishly?

Unfortunately the Professor's report
Has come a bit too late:
I came in this morning and Broadcasting House
Was stamped with a huge sell-by date.

But then, listeners writing to *Radio Times*
(If we take them seriously)
Think it's *always* been stamped with 'Best
Before 1953'.

Graham Chapman

If the British have their own mythology,
It's got to be half Goons, half Monty P.
An Olympus of accountants and Bluebottle,
John Stuart Mill imbibing with Aristotle.
So, from Parnassus Graham Chapman comes;
We fall upon his wit as birds on crumbs,
For comedy, too often, has to claim
'And now for something pretty much the same. . .
And, down the pub or at the office party,
At *every* gathering, there'll be some hearty,
Some homespun star who thinks he has to strut ou
His silly Colonel or his Mrs Cut-Out.
It can't be easy to retain your smile
As silly walks stretch out, mile after mile.
But then, Will Shakespeare too must find it hard;
And who is quoted most, you or the bard?

Roger Law

His Tebbit, Baker, Hurd and Leon Brittan
Are iron-fisted 'neath the rubber mitten,
But he gives, as is natural, pride of place
To the iron mistress of the two-fold face
Which, being rubber, quite appropriately,
Stretches—like her credibility.

A Good Job Too

How often have we heard it asked—
'What do you do then, eh?'
As we sip a tepid Tafelwein
And nibble a canapé.

And at such times, I must confess,
I don't say 'poetry',
Or offer a nonchalant 'writer'; no,
I indulge in fantasy.

I tell them, with an earnest gaze
And firm, trustworthy jaw,
I'm the warm-up man for AJ Ayer
And tailor to Patrick Moore.

Or if they're extra boring and
The wine a bit too chronic,
I sometimes find I'm a spot-welder
For the London Philharmonic;

Or in charge of Round-the-World trips
For the Flat Earth Society;
Or run the Vatican's Mothercare chain,
Or vote for the SDP.

Or if I'm in a satirical mood
And particularly perverse,
I pick the most dead-end of all dead-end jobs
Accountant for a nurse.

But of course there are some ridiculous jobs
That society requires,
Like making translucent plastic coal
To fit on electric fires;

Or local newspaper reporting
Where the proud scoop of the week
Is SUGAR SPILLAGE IN TESCO!
Or MOTHER OF FOUR BUYS LEEK!

10p STUCK IN TELEPHONE BOX!
MAN TURNS LEFT IN CAR!
KITTEN FOUND ON BIRTHDAY CARD:
CHELMSFORD MAN SAYS 'AAAH!'

But perhaps the most useless job of all
The most shaming, the most abased,
Is abridging and gelding works of art
To suit the modern taste.

You know the sort of thing I mean:
The New Classic Selection —
A rose, a dewdrop, a violin
And a licence for vivisection.

They take out all the boring bits
The formal and nutritious,
And leave behind a jelly, flaccid,
Sweet and meretricious.

So now instead of *Belshazzar's Feast*
We're reduced to 'Belshazzar's High Tea'
And the famous Beethoven overture
'Leonora Minus 3';

Britten's 'Single-Combat Requiem',
de Falla's 'One-cornered Hat',
'Bluebeard's Desirable Semi'
And 'The Carnival of the Rat'.

The Dream of Gerontius is forty winks,
A Mass no more than a huddle;
Tchaikovsky's *Swan Lake* has been reduced
To a feather on a puddle.

And the same thing goes for literature —
Browning has faded to beige,
Pope's down to Cardinal, Hardy's gone soft
And Wilde has been put in a cage.

Wholeness, you see, equals dullness; nothing
Now can be swallowed complete.
Soon we'll have the collected poem
Of Wordworth, Yeat and Keat.

And if you think I'm making too much
Of this crass, reductionist habit,
Look at what they've done to Beatrix
Potter's *Peter Rabbit*.

And having found such fertile soil,
Can they bear to leave it there?
The whole of literature is ripe
For a breath of foetid air.

Pugh, Pugh, Barney McGrew,
Dougal and Zebedee
Will help attune us to *Paradise Lost*
By the end of the century.

Watch out for the 'Scratch 'n' Sniff' Ted Hughes
With dead pigs on the cover;
And, later on, the pop–up version
Of *Lady Chatterley's Lover*.

You smile now at my prophecies,
My grim, dark presagings;
But when we, one day, start to lose
On roundabouts *and* swings;

When all the arts lie in the dust
For want of efficient wings,
Then say to yourself 'He was a man
Who used to notice such things. . . .'

Assault by Battery

The world's gone wrong in many ways;
The future's looking bleak.
We grow used to bigots, bullies, bombs,
Politicians' doublespeak;
But society's *really* sick when it buys
Pre-packed bubble-and-squeak.

You may laugh; that's just the tip
Of the iceberg, in a way—
We're sanitized and homogenized
In work and rest and play;
Everything's too easy, bland and
Effortless today.

There's things to save us walking, bothering,
Or communicating;
Peeling spuds or digging weeds,
Thinking, reading, waiting;
And now, from a very early age,
Devices to save us creating.

I refer, of course, to children's toys—
They're extreme to a fault;
Either you get those shapeless, varnished
Lumps of wood from Galt—
All clever and conceptual
And ever so gestalt—

Or else a complex miracle
Of microcircuitry
That's like the credit that you need
To buy it—interest-free:
It walks across the room. Stops. Then
Goes back. Oh ecstasy.

So many are based on TV shows
('The A Team' or 'Doctor Who')
It's hardly surprising if children grow up
Based on TV too—
Assured but empty, and convinced
That 'worthwhile' equals 'new'.

You used to save up for a dinky toy,
For black-jacks, a book or a pen;
Now lasers, blasters, stunners and missiles
Inspire the under-ten;
And the Christmas message is 'Pieces on earth
And good riddance to all men'.

Remember those soft lead farmyard beasts,
Or soldiers for Fort Knox?
Then the wrapping was part of the present, too;
What could be more orthodox
Than to hack and paint and make a boat
Or a farmhouse out of the box?

Now children don't invent, pretend,
Don't draw or build or cook;
The most they ever sit and read
Is an instruction book:
In fact, they don't *play* with toys today—
They press a switch and look.

The imagination's become a vestigial
Organ and atrophies
In this Technicolor, technocratic
Plastic paradise
Where Action Men ogle Sindy Dolls
With their little, swivelly eyes.

Computer games and Speak and Spell
Are typical of the trend;
And that hideous plastic rabbit—pull
A string from its latter end
And that inspires it to confess
That it wants to be your friend.

There's machines to read bedtime stories,
Machines to sing lullabies:
There isn't a pastime you can name
That they can't computerize,
Or geld, or bleed of interest
Or, somehow, dehumanize.

There'll come a time when, up the stairs
You'll creep, to your daughter's bed
And stand beside the pillow where
She's laid her sleeping head;
Her lashes dark as holly leaves,
Her dreams untenanted.

You'll bend and kiss that downy cheek,
Clamped on the tiny thumb;
There'll be a green glow, plastic click,
You'll hear a gentle hum,
And her little dot-matrix will print out
'Night night Dad (oblique) Mum. . . .'

Poem for Margaret

What do you have to do these days
To be chosen for 'Pick of the Week'?
Do you have to be vetted by MI5,
Do you have to join a clique?
Is it best to extrude the satirical tongue
Or keep it in your cheek?

Do we aim for what has oft been thought
But ne'er so well expressed?
Is it anecdotes or recipes
That Margaret likes best?
Or hints on making a budgie-bath
From a Hittite palimpsest?

Oh, Margaret, what constitutes
The best that's on the air?
And do you listen to everything?
Are you scrupulously fair?
Are you a woman at all, my dear,
Or a piece of computer software?

No—I can't believe that that gentle voice
(The essence of Earl Grey tea
And cucumber sandwiches minus the crusts)
Is really a Sinclair Mark III;
But you could be a panel of all that is safe
In the hand-knitted BBC.

I see you in your rocking chair
With dog on cushioned knee;
Antimacassars, brass and chintz
And an ashtray from Winchelsea,
And a copper beech on the leaf-strewn lawn
And Miss Read on the velvet settee.

You have such power, Margaret,
In what you choose to plug;
Whether it's talks on 'The Real Guy Fawkes'
Or 'How to Tame a Slug':
You're the unacknowledged legislator
Of every listening lug.

But I think I've invented an anecdote—
I only wish it were true—
That would find its way on to 'Pick of the Week';
The ingredients are few:
Nostalgia, royalty, tradition and warmth,
And a touch of vulgarity, too.

I'll have to use a rustic voice,
That's a sine qua non:
It sets a comfortable scene
And gives the proper tone
To a narrative so uninspired
That it could not stand alone.

'My father kept a grocer's shop
That catered for the gentry,
With a notice up "Please mind your head
And stoop when making an entry",
And one day he was working on
His fruit and nut inventory

When, outside in the street, he heard
An unaccustomed row,
And, looking up, he saw . . . the King!
And he gulped and made a bow,
And His Majesty stepped through the door,
Consternation on his brow.

"I hear your brother was killed," said he,
"In the war, and I'd like to present
This medal to honour his memory
On my way to a banquet in Kent."
Then he leant across the lemon preserve,
Shook hands, broke wind, and went.'

No, I guess Margaret Howard is like the earth—
Inherited by the meek;
But there is, of course, another way,
The way of the barefaced cheek—
With a final line that reads: 'Until then,
Goodbye from Pick of the Week'. . . .

Never Mind the Quality, Feel the Volume

Look at the way the world has been
Designed for Man's delight,
Mental, physical, spiritual—
The darkness and the light;
With birdsong at morning
And the quiet stars at night;

Proverbial with places where
A pin can be heard to drop,
Where the mind can feed and thought can breed.
We knew it would have to stop,
And it did: in the twentieth century
Someone invented pop.

And now there's muzak punched at us
And spilling all around;
In pubs, in shops, in restaurants—
Even home's not neutral ground
From that hissing, twanging, shrill and slanging
Sempiternal sound;

But neighbours abuse their stereos
Through many an open door;
Never with Bach or Mozart, always
Wham! or Nick Kershaw,
And it shakes the books upon your shelf
And headaches through the floor.

It's the kind of repetition that
Would numb a normal brain—
As if a poet repeated a word
Again and again and again,
And again and again and again and again
And again and again and again.

Those who force their noise on us
Have really got our measure;
'Might is right' is no longer de
Rigueur—but its 'vu' is 'déjà':
Oh yes, we're a democracy now,
So we all have to share the pleasure.

There's video in the post office,
There's the tranny on the train;
There's ghetto blasters in the street;
And in every country lane
Parked cars pump out their Radio 1
With a sound like the smell of a drain.

And now in Guildford, Bromley, Ilford,
Taunton, York, Penarth,
You won't see shoppers smiling and
You can't hear people laugh:
Just an everlasting, blasting
Aural acid bath.

Those worthy men who spend their lives
Making a Bible translation
To suit a passive, lazy, lax,
Self-centred generation,
May come up with a line on Genesis 9
To explain the situation.

I can see it now like a piece of nasty
Grit in my mind's eye:
'The waters receded from the earth,
Lo! All the land was dry,
And God said to the decibel
"Go forth, and multiply".'

So whether you shop in the Arndale centre
Or in Oxford Street,
You won't escape the mental rape
Of the pounding disco beat;
There's litter in the air as well
As litter at your feet.

Complaints appear in papers if
They ring cathedral bells;
There's by-laws about bonfires and
Their sweet, autumnal smells,
So why are we expected to be
Partakers in private hells?

It's worse than additives, Barratt Estates,
Crop sprays, detergents, pylons;
No wonder there's a vogue today
For buying private islands
Where you make the laws and you can cause
An everlasting

A Punch in the Head

The wreckage of the fat tide
Is water-shards in footprints;
The shore lengthens, the day sits inside
Glass. The world is long since.

Children tipped, like tea-leaves
After breakfast, on the hot sand,
Children who were loud and thick as thieves
Sit sulking, islanded in no-man's-land;
A lonely nape of the neck bent,
Daring your touch, your sympathy;
A chip off the old block of discontent
Digging too fast and savagely.

But there, against the promenade's backdrop,
Is a striped tent, like a lollipop
Licked by the breeze,
Where children with sand-patched knees
Crouch, awaiting small atrocities.

There he is, Punch himself:
The hunchback on the shelf,
Unblinking. Dribbling his legs.

While Judy, Toby and the necrophile
Hangman, Baby, Crocodile,
All the partners in this varnished dance,
Leap in glib obedience
To the puppet-master, hand-in-glove
With his stillborn children's vile expedients.

Through nose-like chin and chin-like nose
The scrannel voice that crows
Is the voice of deformity,
Dispensing routine,
Casual enormity;

A new vocal dimension,
An eerie seventh declension;
A klaxon despair, a ghost-train
Wail; the shriek of granite slabs in pain.

Effigy, apparition,
With his too-big, baby head
In the wrong position.

Unhandy, fistless, he clutches his stick
In crossed arms, tight,
As if he clutched a pain,
Crooning his nightmare
Over and over and over again.

The audience look up; too few to speak;
Eyes wide, a sandfly on one downy cheek.

He'll wind and drop inside these heads
Lurid time-bombs, Punch's eggs,
Spinning sickly like a helter-skelter
To explode at Grimm bedtimes
Far inside the Hans Andersen Shelter.

Hatched, he'll mutter syllables of night,
Knock on doors at owl-light,
Approach on non-existent feet
As loud as a heartbeat
In terrible and endless privacies.

His is the dreadful face beneath
The dreadful, hanging dressing-gown; the teeth
That grin as wide as sin, as white
As whey-faced moons.

Ssh! Here he comes, jolting,
In a coat as red as pills.

Cocks his dead eye like a chicken
And then kills.

The North Wind Doth Blow, and We Shall Have a Cold Front Moving Eastwards across the Country Bringing Scattered Snow Showers over High Ground

When snow and poets meet, it makes
For tweeness, on the whole:
All 'fairies', 'magic', 'dancing flakes',
And a lot about 'the soul'—
They ought to spend one January
(At least) delivering coal.

A snowscape from an ivory tower
May seem quite poetic,
But it's less than a winter wonderland
To those who are peripatetic:
Immense, immuring, immitigable,
And, after a while, emetic.

The scenario is always the same:
A few days of flurry and eddy,
And everyone says 'how nice!'; and then
It comes thick and fast and steady,
And the council wakes up and wrings its hands
And bleats that it wasn't ready.

And cars break down by motorways
And are filmed for the news by plane;
And the M1 madmen rediscover
The overturning lane;
And everyone's diesel fuel starts
To wax—and will not wane.

And schools close down, and roads close up;
There are tragedies and farces;
And, only a week or so too late,
The gritting lorry passes,
Breaking the hold of the ice, and several
Senior Citizens' glasses.

And yet . . . there's something about the snow
And its mischievous volte-face;
You know it's snow—when you wake—by the glow,
But there's still the coup de grâce
When you 'huuuhhhhhh' away the tracery
From the window's unstained glass

And the syllables of tree and field
Are mispronounced with snow;
The world's a new, bald statement
Punctuated by a crow.
England's anagrammatized
And Albion's albino.

And elderly ladies slither home
From the January sales,
Arms half-dead and legs wide spread
Like a milkmaid with her pails;
And dogs trot by in a cloud of breath
And cats on a bed of nails.

Snow turns (like a negative)
Translucent to opaque;
Snow turns hares to tortoises,
A car into a cake;
A stroll to an expedition, and
A sprain into a break.

And children take it to their hearts—
And bestow it where they can—
And (undiscriminating souls)
They build their *white* snow*man*
Before its smooth royal icing turns
To yellow marzipan.

Small rustic guerillas,
They hide under heavy hedges
And build up snowy stockpiles from
A dozen window-ledges;
Or raid a potting shed or two
And drag off makeshift sledges

To polish every hillside—seeing
Who can fall off most;
Then home to vermilion firesides,
To tea and buttered toast,
With snow caked on their gaberdines
As if they hugged a ghost.

And I, as the winter evening falls,
Take half an hour or more
To slither my way from the corner shop
Back to my own front door;
While the neighbours stand with cards in their hand:
5.1, 5.1, 5.4. . . .

The Greeks Had a Word for It

Time was when fears were overcome
By rational explanation;
Now they're classified as facts
Which removes all such temptation.

Time was when someone's soft 'There, there!'
Would help when you were scared;
Today 'a trouble halved' means filed
And classified, not shared.

That's all of a piece with a world that's grown
Less personal, more cynical;
The fears we were helped to outgrow are now
Called 'phobias'—that's Clinical!

Your understandable dislike
Of shopping in the rain
Is classed as 'pluviophobia'
With its hint of the insane;

Soon you won't be able to wrinkle
Your nose at a della Robbia
Without some nutter classing it
As terracottaphobia.

And just look at the words they use
As 'phobia' prefixes,
To express each dread from unsliced bread
To fielding Botham's sixes.

There's trypano, vitrico, septo and sphekso,
Cryo, syngenoso, frigga,
Osphresio, lycanthro, lachano, carno—
Don't go, the list gets bigger:

Boustro, cometa, hedyso, agora,
Fechteno, leuco, genu,
Anupto, arachno, myco and conistra,
Dino and ligyro too.

Calypro, hylopho, herpeto, pterno,
(Claustro and hydro you know);
Atelo, botano, psellismo, icono,
Typhlo and coimetro;

Selacho, myrmico, oneiro, ornitho,
Threnoto, dendro and so on;
Cacisto, melano, ichno, isoptero—
If that's not sufficient to go on

There's demo and equino, epistagmo,
If you're getting bored, I'm sorry:
There's still chirapto, catapeda,
Enete and chore.

And that's not all by any means
Collected for you here;
There's scores I haven't mentioned.
Shall I go on? No fear. . . !

There's nothing—well, apparently—
That people aren't afraid of:
Frosts and Fridays, long hair, spinach—
Whatever are we made of?

Surreal as these phobias are,
We might extend the list
And make it quite exhaustive so that
None feels he's been missed.

Parvuscummagnophobia—that's
A fear of bad comedy acts.
Commentatórlogomóribundphobia—
A fear of efficient syntax.

Ambulohominiphobia—that's
A fear of Walkmen and such;
Viamhowardiiphobes are those
Who find 'Howard's Way' too much.

There's probably Oompapaphobia, too:
A fear of the Salvation Army;
And Alistairburnettophobia, which is
A fear of being too smarmy.

There's hibernocanaliphobia—fear
Of what winter does to your guttering;
And, of course, there's phaphaphobia—that's
A morbid fear of stuttering.

There's vialatrinoinversoinventor-
Poculaphobia, too:
That's a fear of finding a cup upside-down
While on the way to the loo.

All these fears are pretty bad.
There is one, though, that's worse:
Nigelocleverdickfordiophobia—
A fear of insipid light verse.

Summer Visitors

This is August, this is London:
    See the sun-tanned, crew-cut head
With jaws in transatlantic motion
    Bending to the *A to Z*.

'Downing St? That's where King Henry
    Knighted Nelson on the Hoe
After Runnymede was conquered
    By that Scotsman, Rizzio.'

Yes, the city's treasures lie here
    Waiting to be marvelled at;
Works of Wren and works of Shakespeare,
    Harrod's, Heals and Habitat.

London looks (like York or Stratford)
    Old only above the waist;
Down below it's plate-glass windows,
    Bulging tills and dubious taste.

Matrons with their wood-grained faces
    Rainmate, talons, henna'd hair,
Clutch their English gift-shop prizes—
    Tweed and hideous chinaware.

Oh, come to London, grand, historic;
    Step back into yesterday:
Donne and Johnson, Keats and Dickens,
    Liberty and C&A.

Standing where the Great Fire started,
    Elmer gives his gum a turn,
Gazing at the stone and brickwork
    Wondering how the stuff could burn.

National Theatre, National Gallery,
    Then the Tate, near Pimlico;
Can't find Shakespeare's birthplace, but
    There's still another month to go.

Another month—of Piccadilly,
    Soho, Strand and Oxford Street;
Moaning at the rain on Monday,
    Tuesday, groaning at the heat.

No standard flies above the Palace,
    Parliament is in recess;
And when you've seen one changing of the
    Guard, you've seen them all, I guess!

Perhaps some cricket, then? A test match:
    Very English—should be fun!
So they spend a whole day searching
    For The Oval, Kensington. . . .

If an Englishman, in glasses
    And a mack against the rain,
Saunters past, they jump and gibber
    'See that guy? That's Michael Caine!'

Evensong—and in the place where
    Charles and Di were married, too;
Lead us not into temptation,
    Lead us back to W2.

This is August, this is London,
    Mistress of a thousand charms;
Not the least, to see the Old World
    With the New World in its arms.

Please Dispose
of this Poem Thoughtfully

For Ivor Cutler

'Rubbish'—not an abstruse word,
But it joins a long, long line
Of others, such as 'Progress', 'God',
'Love', 'Life' and 'Wittgenstein'
As being among the hardest words
In English, to define.

It's anything from earwax to
The family heirloom;
It's something that, despite all threats,
Veneers the children's room;
It's something quite unwanted. Ah—
Unwanted, though, by whom?

Just as one man's meat (proverbially)
Poisons other men,
What X calls rubbish is often in-
Dispensable to N
Whose own offscourings Z will hoard. . . .
And so we go round again.

Just fill a skip with all that family
Dandruff from the attic,
And watch the jackals carting off
Boots, bedsteads, bungled batik;
Like politics, it's rubbish, yes,
But, by gum, it's democratic!

Try buying a Bach manuscript today—
Yet one commentator is certain
They were used as degradable sandwich-wrappings
For students in Anhalt-Cöthen:
That's BWV a hundred and three
To 940 all gone for a burton.

And is it clear that every Vermeer
Is suitably adored?
Hung in a temperate gallery
And lovingly restored?
Or is some pragmatist somewhere using
One as a chopping board?

Oh, rubbish changes—well, butterflies
Spring from caterpillars;
Firelighters today are yester-
Day's best-selling thrillers.
And rubbish ends in November. After
That it's called stocking-fillers.

There's rubbish, too, that's handed out
By highly-salaried men
Who come out with solecisms such as
'Now the main details again. . . .'
Gradually widening the rift
Between 'Homo' and 'Sapiens'.

There's Russell Grant-y rubbish, too:
All those who were born in March—
Your lucky man-made fibre's nylon,
Your lucky tree is larch;
Your lucky stone is gall, your lucky
Carbohydrate, starch.

It's in the second-hand bookshops that
The saddest rubbish is found:
Labours of scholarship, pride or love
That never got off the ground.
Now dull, despondent, dog-eared, damp—
Fourpence each or thirty a pound.

I dedicate this poem, now,
To all that's rubbishy:
To everything that Botha says,
To most that's on TV
To Mills and Boon, to modern hymns,
EastEnders, instant tea;

To jazzed-up Mozart, neon signs,
To the airport paperback;
To jokey sweat-shirts, jelly marmalade,
Fluffy dice, muzak;
To children's annuals, adult films,
To the cheap, the crass, the slack.

Envoi

And after all that, I suppose you're entitled
To ask what I do with my rubbish;
Well, after due consideration,
I rather think I'll publish.

What's the Difference?
or
What Indeed!

Dressmaking and haberdashery
Have a lot in common with Ogden Nashery;
If, after trying it on and twisting it round and breathing in
     and making faces in the mirror and muttering under
     your breath, you find that it still doesn't fit,
You just take it up a fraction or, alternatively, let it out a bit.
Such a practice is generally regarded as having an effect
     which is quite calamitous
On tidy, respectable, English iambic pentamitous.
I am, however, going to copy it,
However sloppy it.
And maybe I'll even dare wreck a
Perfectly good relationship with all my friends in the United
     States of Amarewrecka,
By having the effrontery
To make gentle fun of all and sontery.
But, after all, you can't expect a man who can possibly trace
     his ancestry back to Xiuhtecutli
To agree with an English chartered-accountant absoliuhtecli.
Americans may be fond of calling any man they meet, even
     an English one, 'brother',
But, actually, they are one thing and we are, distinctly,
     another.
Their sense of humour is Walt Disney and Woody Allen,
     avowedly;
Ours is more Oscar Wilde and Noel Cowardly.

The English see Americans as a nation of multi-millionaires
Who think that everything in America is the greatest and
    what's more, it's all theirs;
While we'd have gone bust
Without the National Trust.
The Americans see the English as tweedy, weedy and
    parochial—
As reserved as a railway seat, but at the same time, horribly
    hokey-cochial.
For an Englishman to talk to an American is like receiving
    blow after blow in the solar plexus;
Well—even talking to a Geordie adversely effexus.
And there is, too, the pre-packed, deep-frozen convenience-
    food aspect of the dietary circus:
The Americans have a strong Constitution and can swallow
    old ham with Weinburgers.
Owing to the exigencies of language, an American is
    someone who can answer the doorbell in his vest and
    pants
And still not run the risk of offending the sensibilities of
    anyone on the doorstep, even if they should be
    particularly straight-laced maiden ants.
If an Englishman were to try it
There'd be a riot.
To an Englishman it is nothing short of entirely and
    deliberately perverse
To call a pavement a sidewalk, a road a pavement, a bonnet a
    hood, a gangster a hood, a dressing table a dresser, a
    dresser a bureau and a handbag a purse.
But then, the English are traditionally head-in-the-clouds,
    Keatsy, Shelley and Byrony,
While the Americans are still learning about I Ronnie.
One of the reasons that their language is in demise
Is that they can't resist ending fifty per cent of their words
    with the suffix '-ize'.

The English are conservative and employ a more elegant
     periphrasis;
An Americanism, over here, still stands out like a desert in an
     oasis.
On the other hand, they spell words such as 'color', 'honor'
     and 'valor' in a way which is etymologically true;
We tend to think that such spellings are non-U.
They have worked out that if you add the suffix '-gate' to any
     noun, it signifies something scandalous;
Which provokes the question 'Do we handle the language, or
     does their languagegate handalous?'
The main difference, I suppose, is that the Englishman is
     used to antiquities and relics of the past, so that even if
     he saw a particularly interesting example he wouldn't
     sell his coat for it;
Whereas an American would vote for it.
Children seem to love American things, and I don't mind
     pointing this out since it won't stop my poem working;
For children also love tying bangers to dogs' tails, chewing
     gum, reading mindless comics, eating condensed-milk
     sandwiches, listening to Elton John and watching
     EastEnders when they should be homeworking.

Great Mysteries
of the Twentieth Century

Man is a lover of the unsolved,
Of myth and mystery:
The Marie Céleste, the Pyramids, all
The riddles of history.

The Bermuda Triangle, Borley rectory,
UFOs, Standing Stones,
Atlantis, Glastonbury Tor—
They thrill his modern bones.

There are questions he can answer, there
Are puzzles that he can't;
He can send a man to the moon, but there's still
No cure for Russell Grant.

But there are some modern questions
That tease the probing mind:
Chinks in that mystic curtain which
We long to see behind.

Why does the rain always blow in your face
Whichever way you're walking?
Why do children rub sticks along railings?
Who *chose* to live in Dorking?

How did James Joyce find the time
Among all his op. cits.
To compose the instructions on Tax Returns
And DIY kitchen kits?

Why do we always find blue and white china
Whenever we dig the garden?
Why does glue stay wet on a shoe
But, on fingers, take seconds to harden?

Why does the queue that you join at the bank
Or the Post Office, move like a glacier?
So you're always at least four people away
From that steamed-up, soundproof fascia?

And why, when you cross to a different queue,
Does the one that you've resigned
Go from 0-60 in 45 seconds
While yours gets left behind?

Why do people always shake
A tumbler full of ice?
Why is relaxing so exhausting?
Why are wasps and lice?

Why is there always a deathly silence
When you turn on Radio 3?
Why don't sociologists use
Words from the dictionary?

Why are children accused of 'making a mess'
When their paintings are soggy and smeared;
When Jackson Pollock does the same,
He's hung in the Tate and revered.

Why is *Sunday Sport* called a newspaper?
Has it no sense of shame?
Why is Benny Hill called a comedian,
Or football called a game?

Why do motor mechanics everywhere,
In Staffs, Notts, Yorks, or Beds,
Start every job by sucking in breath
And slowly shaking their heads?

Why has the ugly, the cheapskate, the bland,
What used to be called 'decay',
Done a semantic somersault
To be known as 'progress' today?

Why do your amp, your tuner and deck
Spurt with electrical fires
One and a quarter minutes after
The guarantee expires?

Why are originals *that* sought-after
And forgeries such an affliction?
Why aren't British Rail timetables
Catalogued under 'Fiction'?

Why can't tabloids say 'approve'
Instead of 'rubber-stamp'?
Why can't somebody design
A beautiful standard lamp?

Why, in a language so rich in rhyme,
Is there no rhyme for 'silver'?
. . . . .ah. . . .

The Poet at the Breakfast Table

You won't find many references
In the poetry archive
To food: blancmange, or fish and chips
Or cottage cheese with chive;
Though Keats—we know—was fond of Brawne
And tripe kept Southey alive.

However, thanks to the Bodleian and
Some University Colleges,
I've discovered some Odes to Breakfast which don't
Appear in any anthologies;
Unknown works by well-known poets,
To whom—apologies.

Breakfast with Lucy
by William Wordsworth

I rode among the untrodden ways,
Untrodden up till then:
They wouldn't be untrodden if
I went that way again.

My horse moved on, I moved on too
For I was on its back;
A trick I worked out long ago
And now I've got the knack.

My stomach rumbled and my spirit
Failed for lack of food;
I longed for Lucy and her cot,
Both ill-thatched, low and rude.

And as my horse cropped shoots of grass,
The breakfast he loved most,
There flashed upon my inward eye
Hot plates of buttered toast.

What fond and wayward thoughts will slide
Into a hungry head:
'Oh, mercy!' to myself I cried,
'What if we're out of bread!'

I searched the hedgerows round for fruit
I scanned the dales and hills;
No apples, nuts or berries there—
Just bloody daffodils.

But Lucy waited by her fire
With steaming mug of tea,
Bacon, eggs, fried bread and oh
The difference to me!

And Breakfast Shall have the Dominion
by Dylan Thomas

Once below a time, I, hungry, ran for breakfast through the
     crowing daylight
In the midwiving morning, bones broken of sleep;
    Face honoured among flannels
     Ears washed-behind, I
    Flung stairs over heels and came
Where the whiskered and ramshackling grandfathers
     snapped, crackled, popped
With a dribble of wool-white milk from the farm on the
     harp-shaped hills;
    And fat held green bacon frying
    And it sang in the pan like the sea.

All breakfast long it was sausage, it was toast;
Tomato; nippling mushrooms naked as the field was young;
    And the egg, it was runny
     It was jelly, it was nasty,
    And bacon, oh, Bible-black and burning
Like minstrel logs; and the kettle whistling archangels
In the sabbath steam of the loud and lovely kitchen.
    Breakfast let me play and be
    Golden in the baking of its beans.

To A Breakfast
by Robert Burns

Yon feitlich glourie's gleyn aboot,
We hae the meikle lum, nae doot,
Wi' stammergasted blonkie's hoot
At breakfast.

Wi' kye and ashets timbled too
Nor pipe nor tullet scrails sae true,
Slogged under wi' a skean dhu
At breakfast.

Oh caulie weems ilk reechie bird
Tae pillitch on the selty curd;
I didna understond a word,
At breakfast.

A Midwinter Night Mare's Tail
by William Shakespeare

Prologue

IMAGINATION   What's man but a prisoner? This domestic orb
But a motion'd grave, a glassy interval
Twixt Birth and Death? Cloddish ambition's
No more than dream, and dies diurnally.
Only my Art hath pow'r to mitigate
The staleness of this cabinn'd promont'ry;
No joys hath man—as Mirth, Hope, Wisdom,
Wit—
But from Imagination do derive.
Therefore, as Prologue to this Antic Tale
Come I, Imagination, with sunk cheek
And darkest weeds. Now, gentles, pray you
listen,
For I'm not in the Folio edition.
Wing, then, your thoughts unto a distant isle
Where, lately shipwrack'd on a barren coast,
Comes Ludo—only damp about one knee:
His costume's borrowed from the RSC.
Then comes his bosom-friend, young Domino,
King of Deliria, weeping for his friend
Whom he thinks drown'd and lost, like fair Canasta
To whom he was betrothed and whose sister
Ludo, in like manner, was to wed.
But to untie all knots would mar our tale
Which now we will unfold upon this stage;
The lucid plot sometimes, perchance, will
muddy—
'Twas meant not for examination study.

A Sea Coast

DOMINO Ho there!

LUDO Who calls?

DOMINO A voice! Or do mine ears
Buzz still with horrible imagin'd hum
And clamour of that heavier element
That they were laved withal? Ho there I say!
Aye, yet methinks this 'ho' might be some hope
For presently 'tis half way there, and lacks
But letters two or 'twould be 'hope' indeed.
Marry, and 'twould go yarely with the world
Should every half that lack'd supplied be
To that which, by itself, were nothing worth
Until supplied with the half it lack'd
And made no lack by thus supplying it
with . . . what it lack'd . . . Ho there! who's
within?

LUDO A friend, sir.

DOMINO What! A friend?

LUDO Aye, sir.

DOMINO Speakst sooth?

LUDO Aye, sir, no foe.

DOMINO No foe, thou say'st?

LUDO No sir.

DOMINO Why then, a friend!

LUDO A friend indeed!

DOMINO Stand forth!
What alchemy is this that from base lead
To dearest gold can so translate my heart?
Is't so? Can't be? Aye, still my frenzied brain
Those humours that in blood commingled are
Doth so perplex and enfantasticate
That I durst swear this were no counterfeit
But in that claggy vesture find enlapp'd
My dearest friend. My Ludo. Speak!

LUDO   My Lord. . . .

DOMINO   Tis so! The very aspect of his face:
Same eyes, same hair, same teeth, same
    everything!
No more amazement or my heart, o'ercharged,
Will through its bony cage some exit make.
Ah, poor philosopher, it knows no shift
Twixt joy and sorrow, but alike to each
Plays spendthrift with its sighs; as now it does
Whelm'd with this neap of love; did, heretofore,
Grip'd and envenomed with a serpent grief
That my Canasta's banishment did hatch.

LUDO   Fie on't!

DOMINO   Dost thou remember, coz, what pinch'd
And yeasty looks mine uncle clapp'd on me
When, at the King, my father's death, the crown
In contrary tradition of our house
Fell not to him as eldest of the line
But me alone in unconfederate sway,
Legitimate issue of that second bed,
And latest, that Monopyle, my dam
Shar'd with my father in his solid days?
Thus, dowager'd, undiadem'd and unkind
Most wretchedly he snatched away that prize
Gainst which an hundred crowns were nothing
    worth—
My sweet Canasta, and his child!

LUDO	Fie, fie!
DOMINO	But thou know'st this, my Ludo.
LUDO	Fie, I say!
DOMINO	And thou know'st too how thy love was cut off.
LUDO	Oh, fie again!
DOMINO	I rack our friendship's birth

DOMINO   I rack our friendship's birth
When I do think that twas through love of me
That thou to play the gooseberry didst scorn
And, by degrees

LUDO   O dear degrees!

DOMINO   Didst learn
To love her sister, Halma; banish'd too.

LUDO   Say, shall we sit upon the ribby sands
And with salt tears make increase of the deep
Which, thus augmented, would o'ertop the isle
And drown us in our grief? Come, let's away!
Drab fortune's wheel may turn before the day!

Exeunt

Another Part of the Coast

HALMA Nay, good Canasta, I'll no further. Here
Where nameless buds and blossoms, no less fair
For lack of name, nod to the portly winds
And lose their maidenheads, let's yield our
    names
And all gross Nature owes to selfhood; here
Forsake, and without pain, that which to bear
Were pain eternal.

CANASTA   Thou dost make me, coz,
Almost to waver in my strict opinion
And to break faith with faith that most in bonds
Of indisseverable juncture should be held.
No more of this as you love me.

HALMA   Would I had
That stern heart of yours that might engird
My woman's frailty to endure this isle,
This banishment, this all-unLudo'd place.
But sorrow's wedded to this wilderness
And breeds a parchy desert in my soul
Until it howls for water;
So while I live I'll weep.

CANASTA   And while you weep
Shall fecund Nature spurn her greenness too?
Say, shall this wat'ry orb suck up her seas
And rob the shores to give the clouds increase
All to befit thy humour? Nay, sweet Halma,
Rather should every season smile on you
In hope to make a mirror in your brow
That soon should learn to recompense that
    smile;

Else were each primrose drown'd in every
  shower
That spring had meant to give it best increase.
Troubles come like bees, but, welcoming the
  sting
So we remove the poison and transform
To nectar what were else a deadly shift.

HALMA What! Was sweet medicine e'er restorative?
Is it not rather that the hated draught
Is swiftest purgative?

CANASTA Aye, so I say
Were only she that drinks persuaded so.
For never yet was such a cure performed
With spirit unconformed to the end.

HALMA Oh heavens! Is this Canasta still the same
That once vow'd love, life, honour, every thing
That heart holds dear, unto her Domino
As I to Ludo did with self same sighs?
Can it be she? Oh but what alter'd breast
Contains that heart; and what expansive vows
They were that could expand thus and deny
What first they did avow. I'll stay no more;
My marriage bed I'll make upon the tide;
Never so gladly went so sad a bride.
          Drops her cloak and exits

CANASTA Oh, this is folly! I will after her
And pluck her back again. Do thou lie there—
          Drops her cloak
I must away and check this mad despair.
          Exit. Enter Domino

DOMINO See how my princedom serves me on this isle!
        Were I a beggar I should catch me fish,
        Set me a springe for woodcocks, pluck up roots,
        Find wholesome berries; but I know not how
        And so must starve: I have my breeding still,
        But lack my bread. Degree and worthiness
        Are often opposites that should be twins.
        Kings turn to nothing if they are not fed
        And peasants alive are more than princes dead.
        Come! Whelks shall be my banquet—out, vile
              jelly!
        But stay . . .! This cloak . . .! And this . . . Ah!
              my poor legs
        Play not the jellyfish! And be not thou
        Embutterflied, my belly! It is hers!
        Then is she drown'd, and Halma too; both dead.
        I'll wear this ever for my true love's sake;
        Give this to Ludo, though his heart should
              break.
                  Exit leaving his cloak. Enter Persil, a spirit

PERSIL What folly love in mortals doth devise!
        How are they mocked, how are they punished!
        True love did never enter by the eyes—
        It always starts much further from the head!
        Persil my name y-cleped is. Fear not;
        From surf and tide these lovers I'll defend
        And, by my art, wind up the wand'ring plot.
        But since I rule this island, 'ere the end
        I'll higgle-piggle so these mortal minds
        That much ado they'll have to know
              themselves.

And yet I'll do it in such merry kind
As only Queen Titania's midnight elves. . . .
But hark! I hear the tread of two dull fools
Who on this barren strand long years have spent;
I'll intricate our lovers with these mules
And use false wit to end false banishment.
In shape of some vile monster I'll appear.
Tis done! My magic draws the hempens here.
Hides under Domino's cloak. Enter Scrabble and Cheat

CHEAT Nay, I'm for home too an I could but smell out
the way. Sirrah Scrabble! Faugh, I had rather be
a flea upon a French bratchet than endure these
fogs.

SCRABBLE No fog but a mist, for we have missed our
mark!

CHEAT Why, thou whoreson turnip, thou unlettered
vegetable, wilt thou philosophise? Come!
Where is the bottle? My thirst is inaugurate.
Give me the sack I say!

SCRABBLE Nay, good master Cheat, if I give thee the sack I
fear thou wilt be fired, for your sack is a great
scorcher of the bowel.

CHEAT Go to, go to! Whittle away at thy wit; perchance
it will bring forth good summer mackerel.

SCRABBLE No mackerel but a codpiece and a rare fustian to
jump a joint-stool withal!

CHEAT Eh? What say'st thou? Dost thou decline to
rhetoric? Address me again and I will answer thy
suit.

SCRABBLE Faith, and I will dress you again, if this suit will
answer.

Picks up cloak revealing Persil

CHEAT   A very preponderant riposte; I would
        as soon varnish a Dutch Boatswain as chew
        upon fennel with the wind in that quarter.

SCRABBLE   It doth hang upon thee like Tewkesbury
           mustard upon a neat's foot.

CHEAT   O, mine eyes! They multiply! What have we
        here?

SCRABBLE   Tis thou or I, for there is none but us upon the
           island.

CHEAT   Stand to. I will inspect it consciously.

SCRABBLE   Ay do so—by long division.

CHEAT   What is thy humour? *(kicks it)* Sanguine. Tis of a
        size. Aye, of a most definite size. Well, fellow,
        what art thou worth?

SCRABBLE   No more than a sheal'd peascod I'll warrant. But
           enquire its parentage.

CHEAT   That linear interrogation I'll give to thee, good
        Scrabble, for now I see it is most prodigiously
        toothed i' the jaw and were like to chew a man
        for a pennyworth of sack.

SCRABBLE   Nay then, I'll play the partridge, for I'll be
           hanged 'ere I'll be eaten.

CHEAT   Thou sayest true, for your sea monster is a very
        Tartar for his teeth.

SCRABBLE   Aye, and a very Welshman for his breath. He
           doth lie i' the nostril as high as a hedge-pig in
           Lent. I'll run.

CHEAT   Though thou art legg'd like a hare thou art
        brain'd like a shrew. Strike him, then, for I'll
        none of it. He is a very stretch-mouth'd rascal
        that would break a foul gap in a man's anatomy.

SCRABBLE	Do thou prick him then, for thou art no man and thus 'scape the reckoning.
CHEAT	Nay, that's true, I am no man but a lion for my valour.
SCRABBLE	A lion indeed, for when thou say'st 'I am a lion' thou liest. Go to! Prick on!
CHEAT	Marry, and should cry 'Tailor' or wit's a slow woodworm!

Kicks the beast which roars and they take fright

SCRABBLE	This immoderate exclamation would go nigh to a man's knees and make them but whey; and this way will I take!
CHEAT	Go to, go to! Ay, marry, and I'll go too!

Exeunt

PERSIL	Thus have I my plot begun to weave; Now Halma from her death will I reprieve And bring her sire, Compendium, here as well. I must be gone—but only for a spell.

Exit. Enter Halma and Canasta from the ocean

CANASTA	Once more unto the beach, dear friend, once more: Come let me wrap thee in this cloak.
HALMA	Oh sister! Am I not drown'd? Tell me if I do live Or dream; for as the waters lapp'd me round I dream'd I thought, or thought I dream'd— perchance I but bethought me that I thought methought, Or so I think me now....
CANASTA	What sister?
HALMA	Why,

My Ludo on this island!

CANASTA   Thought you so?
Her heart is sorely charg'd. Come! Rest you here
Within this bosky thicket where the sun
May suck the vapours from thy drippy weeds
And give thee sweet repose. Those humours too
Suck dry, that interfuse their spider pow'rs
And web foul phantoms in th'oppressed brain,
Startling the sense.

Enter Cheat, wearing Domino's cloak and singing

CHEAT When that I was a goodman's son
A loaf of bread was but a crumb. . . .
Aye, so the days go; tilly vally. If the worst
would but mend then straw should be stacked
o'Friday and the beadle should go bare.

Lurches towards Canasta

CANASTA Is this a stagger which I see before me?
O snakes and ladders! 'Tis my Domino!

Faints

CHEAT 'Twas ever thus with a maid and a man of my
compunction. This horizontal disposition doth
portend some prodigious licking o' the boots. I
have marked it before.

Enter Compendium, above

But come, mistress—a word. I would export
you to some concourse with me 'ere we come
to't, for I am no rudesby, and though I be
somewhat tinted i'the frontispiece, when

you reach my contents all shall be black and
white.

COMPENDIUM O marvellous and most horrid circumstance!

CHEAT Thou speakest with no motion of the lips!

COMPENDIUM Gadzooks! Oddsfish! O more than dreadful
deed!

CHEAT Nay, mistress, an thou art thus deep i' the
sound-box I'll not finger thy frets. Go to, I'll
play on thee no more!

Exit

COMPENDIUM My banish'd daughter, slain by Domino!
Why should a man kill that which most he
loves?
'Tis a wild thought. Yet I do believe
That my rash choler hath o'erturn'd his mind.
I do repent me of my covetous deed,
Snatching Deliria's crown from out his hand.
What rule, pomp, majesty, what boast of pow'r,
What glozing courtesy of courtly fools,
What brief authority of kingly state
Could recompense the love I lost that day
That I did turn my daughters out o' doors?
And now my sin doth visit me again,
Grown into death and childed with despair.

Enter Ludo

LUDO Fie, fie, old man; give all this weeping o'er.

COMPENDIUM Fie, fie sayst thou?

LUDO Aye fie.

COMPENDIUM That 'fie' I know— Ludo!

151

LUDO   Compendium!

COMPENDIUM   Nay, stand thy ground;
Methinks thou hast scant cause to love me, sir.

LUDO   I loved thy daughter, and for her sake would
Give thee more reverence than thou hast
        deserv'd.

COMPENDIUM Nay, speak me not fair . . . O heavens! What is't
        you hold?

LUDO   Thy drowned daughter's cloak.

COMPENDIUM   Then she is
        dead?

LUDO   Aye, dead.

COMPENDIUM   My Halma dead.

LUDO   Dead, sir, indeed.

COMPENDIUM My sweetest Halma.

LUDO   Dead, sir.

COMPENDIUM   Can it be?

LUDO   That she is dead? Aye, sir.

COMPENDIUM   My Halma.

LUDO   Dead.

COMPENDIUM And Domino hath killed mine other chick.

LUDO   Nay, sir; not Domino!

COMPENDIUM   Aye sir, I say!
There lies she. This thy father did for thee.
I to find Domino my steps shall bend;
O'ershoes in blood, else, will this action end.

                              Exit

LUDO	Or I am mad, or all the world is so
	And mine eyes made the cuckold to my sense.
	It cannot be the truth that I have heard.
	Come, sweet Canasta, in this thicket lie,
	Safe from the curious and unhallow'd eye.
	Puts on Halma's cloak. Takes her off. Enter Halma
HALMA	What? Voices? Ho, there! What's afoot I say?
LUDO	Why, that which makes its jutty prominence
	Below the ankle, lest the leg should fray.
HALMA	Ah! 'Tis my sister Halma—HALMA???
LUDO	Cheat!!
HALMA	But . . . *I* am Halma!
LUDO	Thou hast *Halma's* voice!
HALMA	I'm here and there; I see and am myself!
	But which is I? This is some sorcery
	To make a false divide 'twixt I and me.
	Exit distracted, leaving cloak
LUDO	There's no divide: my eye says this is she,
	And I am me, not her, and us is we.
	I'll after her.

Exit

Enter Scrabble

SCRABBLE	Well, well; if better fortune come not, I'll sow crabs for the baker's shriving and pen my testament in good Latin. Master Cheat were a rare man for a hic haec hoc, and in truth he hath been o' seasons so full of hock that a would hic two nights together. *(Sees cloak)* This cloak is his. But where is the man? The ground is dry. 'Tis of matter, for an he were prick'd he would eftsoons drain away i' the hot season, being ever more sack than sense.

Enter Cheat

CHEAT	Ethiopian! Say'st thou so?
SCRABBLE	Aye, good cloak, and . . . (???!!!) How now, do I discourse with a gaberdine?
CHEAT	I' sooth. Naught else would bear thy prating!
SCRABBLE	Why now I see this mantle hath a good conceit, for I have oft been upbraided for my want of wit. I'll keep thee and teach thee to rail upon my wife.
CHEAT	(*Footing him upon the hams*) Hark, man, thou art inane!
SCRABBLE	Inane, sir? Aye: a dunce. And this cloak is wood.
CHEAT	Wrap it about thee: thus shall the wood come to dunce inane.
SCRABBLE	This is some jest, had I the wit to mark it.
CHEAT	To market? E'en thou hast wit enough for the market, for they sell sheep's brains there by the dozen.

Exeunt

LUDO	The isle is full of noises. Why, what's here? My Halma's cloak! Then she is gone. Oh dear!

Exit

DOMINO	If Ludo's tale be true and Halma lives, Why may not my Canasta? I'll away; Oft doth the foul turn to the fairest day.

Exit

CANASTA	First did I dream my Domino was here; Now durst I swear that I did hear his voice. I'll take this cloak and to the plashy shore, Sighing for sight of Domino once more.

Exit

154

COMPENDIUM One called on Domino. 'Tis him I seek.
Exit

LUDO I am exhausted and can scarcely speak!
Exit

HALMA Whose was that voice? Dare I believe mine ears?
Exit

DOMINO Each time I enter, someone disappears!
Exit

LUDO That form I know! Canasta!
Re-enter Domino

DOMINO   Halma!
They embrace

LUDO   No. . . .

DOMINO Not Halma?

LUDO   No.

DOMINO   Nor I Canasta.
They begin to leave

COMPENDIUM   Wait!
If you have cloaks, prepare to shed them now.

DOMINO Compendium!

LUDO   'Tis Domino!

DOMINO   Ludo!

COMPENDIUM Halma!
Enter Halma

HALMA   Canasta!

CANASTA   Whist!

HALMA   Patience!

LUDO Diplomacy!

DOMINO   Back, gammon, 'ere I snap!

CANASTA Our father's come to forfeit his usurp'd rights
In fair Deliria, Domino, to thee.

155

DOMINO	Is't so?
COMPENDIUM	Aye, Domino; but the tedious tale
	Thou'llt hear anon from sweeter lips than mine.
	All cares, effects and policy of state
	I have this while conferred on Norway's king.
DOMINO	A Norse?!!
COMPENDIUM	A Norse.
DOMINO	My kingdom for a Norse???
COMPENDIUM	The which, at thy return, he'll tender thee,
	As now I do my daughters. Where art thou?

They are already in each other's arms

HALMA	Here, father, where I mean to end my life
	Which ne'er will start till I am Ludo's wife!
COMPENDIUM	Then, Domino, take . . . ah!—thou hast thine too.
	There doesn't seem a lot for me to do.

Exit

DOMINO	Three days and nights told o'er shall bring us home
	Sweet coz—sweet coz, I say . . .? Well, 'When in Rome' . . .!

He kisses Canasta

HALMA	Art thou more man than he? He kisses faster.
LUDO	Come then aside; teach me this skill to master.
HALMA	Nay, thou'llt play false!
LUDO	We cannot well be both
	The truest lover that did e'er plight troth!

Exeunt

DOMINO	What do we need more than each other, sweet?
	Why not live out our days upon this coast
	And leave Deliria to Compendium's sway?

CANASTA For shame, my Domino! Hath this tyrant love
          Usurp'd thy senses? He should rule the heart
          And have dominion o'er none other part.
          Thou art a King, nor would I wedded be
          To one would deem his kingdom less than me.
DOMINO   Why, spoken like a queen, and bravely said!
          Now to Deliria's shores, crown, church, and
              bed!

Epilogue

Thus, wrongs are righted, love hath won the day
And brought us to the ending of our play.
Let us, before we leave, your pardon crave
Sweet Swan of Avon, spinning in your grave;
'Twas meant as tribute, not to vex thy shade—
Thy potent wine against this lemonade.
If aught hath pleased in all this 'Much Ado'
Join hands, as we, and so to all—adieu.